German Recovery
and
The Marshall Plan
1948 – 1952

by
Herbert C. Mayer

With a Foreword
by
Lucius D. Clay

Edition Atlantic Forum
Bonn – Bruxelles – New York

TABLE OF CONTENTS

FOREWORD

To those Americans who were living in Europe after World War II, it soon became evident that the economic recovery of Western Europe could come about only if all the countries of Western Europe were contributing to such recovery. To those of us representing the United States in occupied Germany, it was apparent that Western Europe could not recover if there was an economic vacuum left in Germany. To wait for the unification of Germany for this vacuum to be filled would have indefinitely postponed the recovery of Western Europe. Because of this, the American and British Zones were united in common economic endeavor, and this unification was soon extended to include the French Zone. The combined zones, which were to become the Federal Republic of Germany, were included in the Marshall Plan.

The rapid recovery of the German economy with Marshall Plan assistance was beyond the fondest hopes of those who had made it possible. It contributed materially to the success of the Plan as a whole and, of course, led to the early assumption of full sovereignty by the Federal Republic of Germany, its entry into NATO as a responsible partner, and its inclusion as one of the original countries in the Common Market.

Much has been written about the Marshall Plan, but perhaps no where has a more succinct account been written of German recovery and its contribution to the Plan as in the book by Herbert C. Mayer, entitled "German Recovery and The Marshall Plan 1948—1952". It is an important contribution to the history of the Marshall Plan which deserves to be read by those who are interested in the Plan, and who want to understand fully what were its accomplishments.

July 15, 1969

Lucius D. Clay
General, Retired
U.S. Army

PREFACE

Recovery from the disaster of a major war was never accomplished as fast as the revival of economic life in Europe following World War II. Yet, from 1945 to 1948, the prospects for recovery seemed dim, indeed. It seemed as though no amount of help changed the utter dependence of European nations upon the largesse of the United States. The peoples of the world had fallen into the habit of looking to the United States for help of all kinds, chiefly dollars.

Yet, the change did come and with it amazing progress. The European Recovery Program developed in response to Secretary of State, George C. Marshall's Harvard Address June 7, 1947, came at a crucial time; it was fashioned with wisdom and ingenuity, and rested upon the base of European prescription for its own rehabilitation. Although considerable funds were put into it by the United States, at least an equal amount was contributed to the counterpart funds by the participating nations. Some used the funds to pay off pressing debts, others ploughed their allotments into capital investment to recondition and expand their industrial systems. But whatever the use, in two and one-half years of the Marshall Plan, Europe had changed so completely that it was hard to believe its previous condition. Europe in 1948, harassed by Communist nagging threats and utterly poverty-stricken, changed to a prosperous active economic unit with power enough to help build up NATO to defend itself against Red pressure while it was returning to the position of a dominant economic unit. In this transformation, Germany played a major role.

This brief report tells the story of the European recovery and Germany's part in it. While the major interest is the recovery of Germany, i.e. the Federal Republic of Germany, no treatment of German recovery alone could tell the story completely. The Western European countries had to recognize that they could not rebuild a viable economic system for Europe without Germany; and Germany found out that it could never rebuild its place in the world without its European neighbors. Hence, this is the account, not of German recovery, but of European recovery in which Germany had a major role. Moreover, progress of Germany from

3

a beaten enemy without resources or hope to one of the few outstanding economic producers of the present day, is more than a story of material progress, it is the success story of a people who rose from defeat, and burdened by almost ten million refugees and expellees who had to be provided for, built a new economic empire to become one of the prime movers in the world today. In final analysis, this is the story of dedicated leadership whose wise counsels and sound policies led the people through bitter reconciliation and bitterly hard work to the sweet taste of achievement and comfort. It is no accident that Germany today is a great nation wielding an influence among the world leaders and assisting many emerging peoples, to build their own life and government. Moreover, while German leaders have done an exemplary job of showing their thanks and appreciation for American help, they have demonstrated that the best thanks is passing on what they received to others in need. In many respects, the German assistance to emerging nations rivals that of the United States.

The author was persuaded to write this monograph, not because he is the best informed on European economic affairs, but because he saw what was happening when he was an officer of military government in 1947 and 1948 and has continued his interests in what has been happening to the people of Germany. He agreed to undertake this task because he felt that a better understanding of what actually happened in Germany during the period of the Marshall Plan will lead to better relations between Americans and Germans in the sometimes dangerous times ahead. The subject deserves a more comprehensive treatment, but this may well serve the purpose until someone else does a thorough job.

My thanks go to the staff of the Springfield, Massachusetts Public Library for its efficient aid in finding government documents so necessary to the gathering of vital data, to Mr. Hans D. Wenders who has assisted greatly in getting materials for my use, and to my employer, American Viewpoint, Inc., whose Board allowed me to take a partial leave of absence from my regular duties to devote myself to this project. I must also pay my debt of gratitude to my secretary for whom the typographical assistance has been an extra chore, taken cheerfully, and to my wife whose help in research and aid in the editorial work has been invaluable.

It is my hope that instead of ending the study of this vital subject, this small effort may encourage wider research to master the techniques of recovery from a devastating war, if alas, one might descend upon mankind again.

May 29, 1969

Herbert Carleton M a y e r

Chapter I

THE BACKGROUND OF THE EUROPEAN RECOVERY PROGRAM

The After-math of World War II

Certainly World War II was the most destructive conflict in history; destructive of lives, of property, and of the economic systems of the nations involved in it. When the armistice was finally signed in May 1945 Europe was a shambles. Its peoples were destitute, with little shelter, and with scarcely enough food to keep body and soul together. From Stalingrad to St. Nazaire; from Murmansk to Bengazi the devastation covered Europe, with the heart of the destruction in Central Europe. Manufacturing was paralyzed; commerce was almost at a standstill; people scrounged for whatever food they might find. Only the black market operator prospered. Even if people wanted to rehabilitate their economic life, they had no time left after the effort to maintain existence.

Populations that existed through that post-war period look back upon it today wondering how they ever survived. It truly was an onerous ordeal. Agriculture had to struggle with unexploded bombs and shells in their fields, lack of fertilizer, and the appalling scarcity of seed. Manufacture had ground to a halt, tooled only for war production and machinery worn out and of little use. Such plants as might have some potential were subject to the reparations dismantling program by which victors took replacements for their own losses. Transportation was almost hopeless for bridges were gone and roads and road-beds had been bombed into uselessness. Canals were plugged with sunken barges, and rivers were blocked by fallen bridges. In effect, shipping was at a standstill. Churches, schools, hospitals, theatres and homes were only ruins. Almost every family had lost fathers or sons, and those who came back were frequently debilitated by long imprisonment or disease and wounds. Central Europe was spent, worn out, and for the most part without hope to rebuild.

Occupation Army Aid

The only bright spots were the military establishments of the victorious Allies whose armies had occupied the land and who had the job of maintaining themselves and the desolated territory in their possession. Italy had suffered in the last years of the war; France had experienced the terrors of fighting armies involved in breaking the hold of Hitler's occupation forces. Russia, prostrated by invasion and defeat early in the war, had turned the tide and driven the Nazi armies into their own country but it too had an enormous task of rebuilding. The most recent and perhaps the most violent destruction had occurred in Germany at the time of the final invasion and victory of the Allies.

Wherever the Allied Armies held control they had to repair and rebuild for themselves, and because much of the public utilities were needed the "indigenous" workers were pressed into service not only for allied benefit but also for the German population. Thus the vanquished people of Germany benefited indirectly from the necessary rebuilding and reclaiming of devastated areas for practical use. The degree of help enjoyed by the Germans depended on the occupying army. The Soviets did little that helped the Germans; the French were less severe and the British helped grudgingly but the Americans were generous with their aid. This was true whether it involved clearing streets, rebuilding structures, or providing food.

The American service men were soon spotted as an easy touch by children and adults alike and they shared their food allowances with the less fortunate. Moreover, they wrote home to tell about the pitiful lack of food and clothing with the result that hundreds of thousands of packages came from American families to ameliorate suffering. Before long, each soldier was a sort of informal welfare agency in the areas around him. Inevitably this led to organized relief both by the government and among private organizations. The volume of this aid soon took on major proportions. Representative Sadowski of Michigan in Congressional debate reported that from July 1945 to September 1947 the United States had given Germany and Italy over $ 1,674,000,000; Poland, Czechoslovakia, Finland, Hungary, Albania, Yugo-slavia, Bulgaria, Rumania, and the Union of Soviet Socialist Republics $ 1,644,000,000; England, France and Greece over $ 7,288,000,000 in the same time [1]). In the same debate, Senator Wherry of Nebraska quoted figures showing that 90,000,000 individual packages had been sent to people in Germany, with the government paying the transportation costs on them [2]). Congressman Rich of Pennsylvania reported to the Congress that the United

States had given loans, grants, or credit for relief purposes from 1945 to 1948 the sum of $ 25,495,952,923 [3]). In 1946, the United States Government set up a fund called GARIOA — Government and Relief in Occupied Areas — with funds to deal with the relief problems directly. The Federal Republic of Germany reports that from 1946 to 1950 this amounted to $ 1,620,200,000 [4]).

It was American aid that poured into Europe to keep England and France going during the War, and the same source provided billions to keep millions of people alive after the War. Yet it failed to arouse the fallen spirits to rebuild. The money that was poured into Europe seemed to have no result. It was apparent that this could not go on; some new program was necessary to arouse and stimulate the people of Europe. The United States for all its resources could not go on indefinitely providing charity to keep the impoverished alive.

Origin of the Marshall Plan

It was in June, 1947, in a commencement address at Harvard University, that Secretary of State, George C. Marshall proposed a plan of assistance to cooperate with those European nations that would assume initiative to meet the situation. This led to a meeting of Britain, France and the Soviet Union to plan for some way to meet the challenge thrown out by Secretary Marshall. The Soviets would not go forward with it, however, and the hope that all Europe might be included faded. It might be noted that the Soviets not only refused to participate but also kept Czecho-slovakia, Poland and Hungary from doing so. In September 1947, sixteen nations met to develop a plan of cooperative action to bring about European recovery. Out of their meeting, the Committee of European Economic Cooperation, as it was called, came the evaluation of needs to bring about a permanent solution to the recovery problem. In the meantime, in the United States, a President's Committee on Foreign Aid, European aid, European Recovery and American Aid was appointed under the leadership of the Hon. W. Averill Harriman, then Secretary of Commerce. The Committee was composed of distinguished business and civic leaders in the United States. Its report outlined conditions in Europe and America, indicated limitations and dangers, and gave guide lines for the development of a practical program of limited aid to bring European nations to their feet in four years. It was an influential factor in the consideration of the matter by the Congress, and created a favorable climate of public opinion.

Fundamentals of American Aid

The report of this Committee sets forth the problem so explicitly that it is worth quoting at this point because it outlined the pattern for consideration of American Aid to European Recovery.

"We believe that the future of Western Europe lies very much in its own hands. No amount of outside aid, however generous, can by itself restore to health the economies of the sixteen nations met in Paris in July. Except in Western Germany, where the United States had direct governmental responsibility, the success of any program depends ultimately on the hard work and straight thinking by the people and the governments of the European nations themselves. The sixteen nations and West Germany comprise over 270,000,000 men and women. They possess great agricultural and industrial resources. Even in its present depressed state, the production of this area is vastly greater than any aid which this country can provide. Such aid must be viewed not as a means of supporting Europe, but as a spark which can fire the engine.

"The Committee is also aware that the volume of aid required from the United States is of such proportions that it will place a substantial burden on the people of the United States. For all its resources, the United States is no limitless cornucopia. The population represents something less than 7 % of the population of the world. We have heavy responsibilities at home, as well as in Asia, and in our own hemisphere. The aid which we give represents, to be sure, only a small fraction of our total production, but at the present time, there is no slack in the American economy and every shipment abroad of scarce goods, — especially food which Europe must have, — adds to the inflationary pressure at home.

"The Committee regards as nonsense the idea which prevails to a considerable degree in this country and abroad that we need to export our goods and services as free gifts to insure our own prosperity. On the contrary, we are convinced that the immediate economic danger to the United States is inflation, which means, among other things, a shortage of goods in relation to demand. We believe that we should aim to achieve a condition in which exports from this country are more nearly balanced by a return flow abroad of services and materials essential to our own economy. We also believe that the European nations desire to achieve such an equilibrium in the interests of their own self-respect and prosperity. To make this equilibrium possible should be a major objective of any program of aid. The interest of the United States in Europe, however, cannot be measured simply in economic terms. It is also strategic and political. We all know that we are faced in the world of today with two conflicting ideologies. One is a system in which individual rights and liberties are maintained. The opposing system is one where iron discipline by the state ruthlessly stamps out individual liberties and obliterates all opposition.

"Our position in the world has been based, for at least a century, on the existence in Europe of a number of strong states committed by tradition and inclination to the democratic concept. The formulation of the Paris Report is the most recent demonstration that these nations desire to maintain this concept. But desire is not enough. The democratic system must provide the bare necessities of life now and quickly rekindle the hope that by hard work a higher standard of living is attainable. If these countries by democratic means do not attain improvement in their affairs, they may be driven in turn in the opposite direction. Therein lies the strength of the Communist tactics; it wins by default when misery and chaos are great enough. Therefore, the countries of Western Europe must be restored to a positive position where they may retain full faith in the validity of their traditional approaches to world affairs and again exert their full influence and authority in international life." [5])

Opposition to the Marshall Plan in the United States

While many Americans were aware of the economic plight of Western Europe there was strong opposition to giving further aid to nations which seemed to be unable to work out their own recovery. The never-ending series of crises in Europe and the need for food and the necessities of living had exhausted the sympathy of many Americans. Moreover, millions of service men returned to their homes with severely critical attitudes toward what they saw in Europe and the constant exploitation of the military by civilian shops, hotels and restaurants, abroad. There had grown up in some quarters the feeling that all the blame for the war did not lie with the Germans and Hitler's leadership, that if those nations which had been our Allies had acted positively to the Nazi threat when it was rising there would not have been a war. These attitudes found frequent expression during the debate in Congress, and only the combined efforts of both Democrats and Republicans brought about the passage of the act that set up the European Recovery Program. The leadership of Senator Arthur Vandenberg and Representative Christian Herter especially rallied to support President Truman on this measure.

There was also a bad American reaction to the frequently expressed statement among European leaders that the United States owed them everything they needed because they endured the long rigors of the war. Furthermore, there was American resentment against the steady rise in taxation to provide for the peace-time needs as well as the former demands of the war itself. Perhaps there was also the feeling that many European nations were already socialistic in form.

The economic problems in themselves convinced many business men that the United States should not extend itself further to provide foreign aid. By 1948, the change-over from a war economy had revealed very serious shortages of raw materials and the needed components for manufactured goods. For instance, people wanted to return to rubber again after the war had forced them to be satisfied with synthetic substitutes. Many metals were in short supply, and the oil reserves had been depleted in heavy use during the military and naval operations. Europe was also in need of similar materials, and American industry faced shortages that would impair the production of goods the consumer wanted. The agricultural needs of Europe were far in excess of what American farmers could supply. American industry and commerce wanted to get back to normal production and trade and particularly foreign operations that could mean profit and expansion.

Behind all this economic pressure was the threat of inflation from the pent-up demand for consumer goods and the accumulation of savings during war years. The President's Committee pointed out every shipload of supplies and goods from America meant an aggravation of the danger of inflation which might be disastrous to the United States. And the high taxes, which were accepted during the war, were looked upon as an unwelcome burden now that peace had come. Moreover, many of the older generation remembered the financial calamities that followed the unpaid debts after World War I and they wanted none of that again. Although Europeans might have been unaware of this unfavorable tide of public opinion, the successful passage of the Foreign Aid Act of 1948 was a political achievement of considerable proportions.

Conditions in Germany

So much for the general background, let us now turn to the particular conditions that existed in Germany. The first and foremost fact was the occupation of the country by the four conquering armies and the division of the country resulting from the fact. It is true that the original plans agreed upon at Yalta envisioned a single central organization of military government in Berlin under the Allied Control Council, composed of the four military governors, that is the commanding generals of the occupying forces; but that organization never could function satisfactorily because it had been agreed that all decisions would be made by unanimous consent and the Soviet Union had consistently refused to go forward with measures to re-establish Germany as a viable government, and out of simple necessity the other three powers had found it necessary for each occupying army to undertake steps toward the administration and rehabilitation of its own zone. This meant a situation that was paralyzing in effect, and confusing in its diversity.

The most evident result was the division of Germany into the zones, namely, East Germany under the control of the Soviet Union, and the western zones under the British, French and American armies. The British and Americans soon took steps to unify their activities, with a merger for economic development under the Bizonal Economic Council. Collaboration of the two Military Governments began to produce the beginning of recovery in the British and American Zones. Professor Ludwig Erhard was designated the Director of this unit and under his leadership steps were taken to coordinate efforts to rebuild the economic life of those zones. Aside from the breaking up of cartels and the very large and dominating companies in the steel and chemical industries, the biggest step by this agency was the release of government controls following the currency change on 15 June 1948. This was a major step in rehabilitation of German life.

Until that time, the scarcity of food immobilized all industrial and commercial efforts. Maintaining bare existence took almost all the energy and ingenuity of men and women to stay alive. Their money was nearly worthless because no one knew where inflation would end, and it was not readily acceptable on payment of debts. The entire land was, in practical effect, on a barter basis with all the limitations implied in that form of exchange. In fact, one might say that the only acceptable currency was American cigarettes. The occupying armies had issued their own "occupation currencies" and changed them frequently enough to foil the black market operators. What little trade went on between Germans and occupying personnel was managed through barter for food or cigarettes. The uselessness of the old German currency sprang from the fact that when the occupying powers undertook to print German money to supplement what was in circulation, the Russians insisted on having plates which the American authorities had produced, and foolishly some were given to the Soviet allies. This was a fatal mistake because the Russians proceeded to print unlimited amounts of the Hitler money, and the resulting devaluations made it useless. The only hope for stable economic life lay in getting a sound currency that people could accept and which would represent value. This the Soviets refused to do, and finally on 15 June 1948 the three West Zone Military Governments initiated an exchange that brought the new and stable money system into being. It should be noted that the main side-effect of this exchange was the blockade of Berlin and its dramatizing of the schism between East and West governments.

But the German problem was far more complicated than this over-simplified description. For one thing, Germany had coal, and without coal, Western Europe could not operate. Yet war psychology still dominated, and it was even suggested that Germany be compelled to mine coal and deliver it to the Allies without compensation and without retaining any for herself. Of course, such a course of action was ridiculous beyond

14

belief, and it was never given serious consideration in the Organization for European Economic Cooperation in Paris. Furthermore, Germany had been the industrial center of Europe for generations and after the war its industrial system was in ruins, its sources of supply of raw materials were cut off, and its manpower was disasterously depleted. Yet the OEEC recognized that "the producing and purchasing power of Germany and through Germany the producing and purchasing power of all Central Europe was indispensable to the recovery of Western Europe. Germany's current (1948) production was catastrophically low in view of the great increase in population — only 51 % of the 1938 level. The Committee feels that a quick recovery of the Bizonal area, especially the Ruhr, is of paramount importance to European recovery." [6])

German Progress Essential to Europe

The OEEC concluded its report on special consideration of the German area by stating, "Other Western European nations cannot be prosperous as long as West Germany is paralyzed". Here then was a growing recognition that Europe needed West Germany as much as Germany needed Europe. That was the beginning of a new attitude toward Germany. The Committee went on to say: "It is necessary to achieve a standard of living which will prevent reaction and unrest; it is a vital concern of Britain, France, and the United States to reduce occupation costs by increasing exports from Germany; and at least for a time Germany's output cannot be duplicated elsewhere. Before the War, Europe depended on Germany for metals, machinery and chemicals." [7])

The requirements outlined by the OEEC for Germany's recovery included: 1) Restoration of orderly and efficient administration; 2) Establishment of a unified currency and price system; 3) Removal of pressure on Military Governments to economize their dealings with other countries; 4) Rehabilitation of mining, transport and manufacturing facilities and increase of food rations, housing, clothing and human necessities; 5) Resumption of normal trade relations between Germany and the outside world. Moreover, all observers agreed that normal life in Germany cannot be restored without some form of German Government to handle nationwide problems. The current local and zonal organization developed inevitable confusion and conflict between areas. Ideally, there should have been one Germany covering four zones, but if this was impossible under prevailing conditions, then a start should be made with the three west zones.

The continual pressure for every possible economy in dollar expenditure had delayed the integration of West Germany into the Western European economy. The zonal division had developed artificial policies instead of natural ones. For instance, shipment of United States supplies had all been routed through Bremen and Bremerhaven and then by railroad or truck to the American Zone at high cost, when actually a low-cost water route was readily available through the Low Countries and up the Rhine River. This increased the problem and cost of integrating Germany with Europe.

Again, Europe's greatest problem was coal, and until more coal was mined, Europe could not grow. Yet mining was not the only bottle-neck; transportation was also difficult. Before the War there existed an exchange system for railroad cars; immediately after the war every country seized whatever rolling stock it could lay its hands on with the result that the distribution of cars for freight was badly complicated. If other countries were ever going to get coal, they would have to avoid needless duplication of travel. The need for fertilizer was also bound up in the transportation block, for more fertilizer could be produced only by more coal and more food could not come unless there was more fertilizer. Perhaps the basis of much of Germany's trouble was the scarcity of food. When it is realized that the usual consumer ration in the Bizone in 1947—1948 was 1550 calories, and this was not always met, as compared with a normal per capita calorie ration of 2850 in prewar Germany, it is evident that the food shortage was crucial.

The final conclusion of the OEEC was that external contacts through normal communication and travel must be restored to Germany, if export trade was to be developed. The Committee summarized its position as follows: "Rebuilding German life requires not only financial aid but the human factor of morale and relief from skepticism and economic frustration among German people. The Committee assumes that the United States and its Allies will take steps necessary to effect a vital ending of the resurgence of an aggressive military Germany. The Committee is convinced that Europe cannot be rehabilitated without major recovery in Germany." [8]

[1]) p. 577, Congressional Record, 80th Congress 2nd Session Jan.—Dec. 1948; Vol. 94, Pt 1.

[2]) p. 2187, Congressional Record, 80th Congress 2nd Session Jan.—Dec. 1948; Vol. 94, Pt 1.

[3]) p. 1404, Congressional Record, 81st Congress 1st Session Jun.—Oct. 1949; Vol. 95, Pt 1.

[4]) p. 19, 12th Report of the German Federal Government on the Progress of the Marshall Plan, Pt 1.

[5]) p. 3—4, Report of the President's Committee on Foreign Aid, European Aid, and American Aid. Nov. 7, 1947.

[6]) p. 35, U.S. President's Committee on Foreign Aid, European Aid, and American Aid.

[7]) op. cit. p. 119.

[8]) op. cit. p. 122, referring to the Report of the Committee on European Economic Cooperation, 1947.

Chapter II

THE ORGANIZATION AND POLICY
OF THE EUROPEAN RECOVERY PROGRAM

Developing the Plan

The suggestion by Secretary George C. Marshall that a new form of aid be developed by which the United States could help Europe rehabilitate its economic system was followed by a meeting of representatives of sixteen nations in Paris, the Committee of European Economic Cooperation. This Committee drafted a four year program of assistance aimed at putting each of the nations on its feet and relieving the need of further aid from the United States. The concept was broad but the actual need for funds was not too much beyond the potential of the United States. It had the added merit of decreasing the aid year by year with the goal of complete economic independence. This report was submitted to the President in September 1947 and was referred to the President's Committee on Foreign Aid as previously noted. The proposed bill was submitted to Congress and debate began when Congress convened.

We have already listed some of the recommendations of the President's Committee; there were other studies and reports, including the Krug Report on American Resources initiated by Secretary of the Interior, Julius K. Krug. This undertook to analyze Europe's urgent needs and possibility of supplying them from American resources. For instance: Wheat could be supplied in large quantities as long as the crops remained good; nitrogen fertilizers were in short supply in the United States and production only met national need; coal could be mined but its delivery would be limited by lack of cars; steel was in heavy demand and unless there could be an expansion of production facilities none would be available; industrial equipment was in short supply but some might be available [1]).

The Nourse Report by the Council of Economic Advisers [2]) stated that the United States had financed four-fifths of the export surplus since 1945 and without some further aid program to supply funds, American export, mostly European, would drop from 13 billion dollars to four to five billions. Danger to the American economy was chiefly from inflation. It warned that foreign aid to restore production would bring new competition.

The Summers Report on Economic Aid to Europe pointed out that the United States had left European affairs to the nations in that area and centered its attention upon the countries with urgent needs. Then came the British request for a huge loan and Congress voted it with the assurance that it would put the United Kingdom on its feet, but within a short time that nation asked for more help. Then Greece pleaded for a large loan to save it from economic disaster and France was in grave economic difficulty. The United Nations talked about the problem but it had no funds and could do nothing. Sixteen nations were in serious trouble [3]).

The Committee of European Economic Cooperation

The Report of the Committee of European Economic Cooperation (22 Sept. 1947) described the organization and set up the Paris Conference in Volume I, and the Technical Reports on Needs and Resources in Volume II. The members of the Conference were Austria, Belgium, Denmark, France, Greece, Iceland, Ireland, Italy, Luxembourg, Netherlands, Norway, Portugal, Sweden, Switzerland, Turkey, United Kingdom. Germany was not represented at this conference but was included later. The United States and Canada joined the OEEC as associate members in 1950. As we have noted, the Soviet Union had been invited to the first meeting prior to the Paris conference, but refused to go along with the plan. Czecho-slovakia, which accepted and then was forced to withdraw by Russia; Poland and Hungary were also prevented from joining. Thus, the final membership was composed almost entirely of Western European countries with the exceptions of Greece and Turkey. The quality of the work of this Conference was very high. The representatives devoted themselves to the best interests of Western Europe without undue emphasis upon what their own countries might get. Under the final plan, the same group became the Organization for European Economic Cooperation and continued to exercise an important influence on the whole Program through the years.

The United States Congress passed the Foreign Aid Act on 2 April 1948; President Truman signed it on 3 April; and appointed Paul Hoffman to the Office of Administrator on 9 April. On 15 April the Organization for European Economic Cooperation convened in Paris to take up the final work of determining the needs of the sixteen participating countries. The situation had become desperate and speedy action was a prime consideration. Congress passed the appropriations bill shortly thereafter. The Washington office was staffed and the European unit set up rapidly and the American and British Occupation Zones of Germany were added to the OEEC, as was the French Zone later. By the end of the quarter, 30 June 1948, allotments amounting to $ 1,316,300,000 had been made to the participating countries and $ 738,500,000 in procurement authorization had been approved. Food and needed supplies were coming to Europe. This was possible because the Committee for European Economic Cooperation had done a careful technical job in 1947 and its Report of 22 September 1947 was ready for immediate consideration by the Economic Cooperation Administration (ECA) staff.

Organization of the Economic Cooperation Administration

The bill setting up the machinery to administer the European Recovery Program provided that the Administrator and his staff should be headquartered in Washington; a deputy and his staff for liaison purposes was to have an office in Paris convenient to the Organization for European Economic Cooperation since this group was to be the key European unit in determining the needs and allotments of aid and supplies. Each participating nation was to set up a unit for its own national program maintaining liaison with the Paris headquarters and with an American ECA officer for that country. All operations were to flow through this direct administrative organization.

ECA's operation was simplified to speed up the supplies and services needed. The process is pictorially represented in the accompanying figure, Since the OEEC had prepared the general program of needs and this had been approved in principle by the ECA, there was little need for further review. The purchaser in the participating country, after getting his own unit's approval, made a request for ECA funds in payment for their goods or services under the Grant Aid plan; this went to the

COUNTERPART FUND PROCEDURES

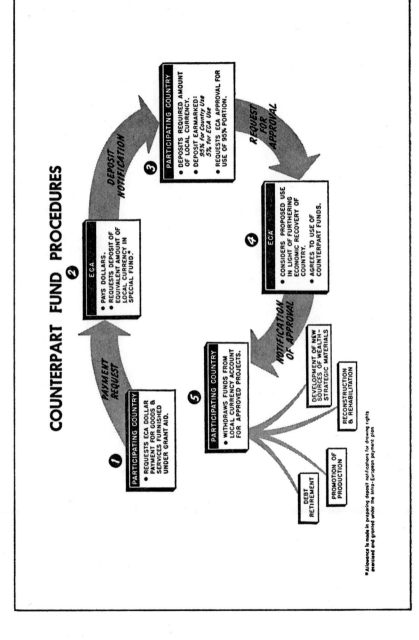

1 PARTICIPATING COUNTRY
- REQUESTS ECA DOLLAR PAYMENT FOR GOODS & SERVICES FURNISHED UNDER GRANT AID.

PAYMENT REQUEST

2 ECA
- PAYS DOLLARS.
- REQUESTS DEPOSIT OF EQUIVALENT AMOUNT OF LOCAL CURRENCY IN SPECIAL FUND.*

DEPOSIT NOTIFICATION

3 PARTICIPATING COUNTRY
- DEPOSITS REQUIRED AMOUNT OF LOCAL CURRENCY.
- DEPOSIT EARMARKED: 95% for Country Use 5% for ECA Use
- REQUESTS ECA APPROVAL FOR USE OF 95% PORTION.

REQUEST FOR APPROVAL

4 ECA
- CONSIDERS PROPOSED USE IN LIGHT OF FURTHERING ECONOMIC RECOVERY OF COUNTRY.
- AGREES TO USE OF COUNTERPART FUNDS.

NOTIFICATION OF APPROVAL

5 PARTICIPATING COUNTRY
- WITHDRAWS FUNDS FROM LOCAL CURRENCY ACCOUNT FOR APPROVED PROJECTS.

- DEVELOPMENT OF NEW SOURCES OF WEALTH—STRATEGIC MATERIALS
- RECONSTRUCTION & REHABILITATION
- PROMOTION OF PRODUCTION
- DEBT RETIREMENT

*Allowance is made in preparing deposit notifications for drawing rights exercised and granted under the Intra-European payment plan

ECA office, where the allotment was made and the national unit was informed of its procurement and notified to deposit the amount of its dollar cost, including shipment freight rate in local currency, in the Special Fund. A deposit notification was sent to ECA and the operation was completed. The funds in the Special Account were earmarked; 5 % for ECA use, and 95 % for use in the country of deposit. When the participating country wanted to use those funds it prepared a request outlining use and needs and submitted it to ECA for approval. On approval, ECA notified the national unit and authorized withdrawal for the specified use. The accepted purposes for such use were: 1) debt retirement, 2) promotion of production, 3) reconstruction and rehabilitation, and 4) development of new resources of wealth producing materials. We should note that in this process the United States through ECA paid dollars for goods and services; while the recipient paid local currency into the Special Account. This eliminated balance of payment difficulties where needy countries had no reserves to pay debit balances. Sources of supply, wherever they might be, would be paid in viable currency. Much of the materials came from the United States and the Western Hemisphere, but the Asian sources were also tapped.

The ERP also encouraged trade between the participating countries and eventually provided a payments union to obviate the difficulties of bilateral trade balances. Later the OEEC undertook to reduce national tariffs and duties discriminating duties against neighboring nations. The ECA and the OEEC also contrived to provide credit for nations whose need was urgent but who had no adequate funds with which to pay for supplies.

Agreements with Participating Countries

The arrangement for each nation was secured by a signed agreement between the participating nation and the United States of America, providing for: 1) The purpose of the ERP; 2) Assistance and Cooperation; 3) General Undertakings; 4) Guarantees; 5) Local Currencies; 6) Access to Materials; 7) Consultation and Transmittal of Information; 8) Publicity; 9) Missions; 10) Definitions; and 11) Entry in Force, Amendment, Duration. Typical of these bi-lateral treaties was the one signed with Bizonia of West Germany by the two Military Governors (see Appendix 1). The letter of Intent was signed on 14 May 1948 and the date of the bilateral agreement was 14 July 1948. There was prompt action on the participation. Austria was the first to sign the letter of Intent on 15 April 1948 and the French Zone of Germany was the last on 3 June 1948.

1948—1949 Allotments

Based upon the previous work which produced the 1947 Report, the OEEC immediately completed its proposed recommendations for the recovery program. The following table outlines the details of the plan:

Proposed ECA Program for 15 Month Period [4])
9 April 1948 — 30 June 1949
(in millions of dollars)

Countries	OEEC Aid Recommended	ECA Aid Proposed	Allotment for Current Appropriation	Supplement to any Allotment Requested
Austria	$ 217	$ 215.2	158.8	56.4
Belgium-Luxembourg	250	247.9	196.0	51.9
Denmark	110	109.1	80.—	29.1
Trieste	18	17.8	14.2	3.6
France & Possessions	989	980.9	723.5	257.4
Germany-Bizonia	414	410.6	307.1	103.5
French Zone	100	99.2	72.3	26.9
Greece	146	144.8	127.0	22.8
Iceland	11	5.2	5.2	—
Ireland	79	78.3	78.3	—
Italy	601	555.5	422.7	132.8
Netherlands	496	469.6	368.0	101.6
Norway	84	83.3	61.8	21.5
Sweden	47	46.6	40.4	6.2
Turkey	50	39.7	34.8	4.9
United Kingdom	1,263	1,239.0	919.1	319.9
Commodity Reserve	—	13.5	13.5	—
Total Program	4,875	4,756.2	3,617.7	3,138.5
Strategic Material		4.6	2.6	2.0
Ocean freight on relief		15.5	11.5	4.0
Technical Assistance		5.0	3.0	2.0
Investment Guarantees		27.7	27.7	—
Administration		14.3	10.8	3.5
Confidential Fund		.2	.2	—
Total ECA Funds		4,823.5	3,673.5	1,150.—

OEEC presented a combined report on the needs of each country: 1) Forecasts of its domestic production, consumption, etc.; 2) Estimates of expenditures to be made for imports of essential goods and services and of earnings to be derived from sale of exports; 3) Incomes and expenditure statements giving its estimated foreign trade position. The OEEC gathered these and ECA received them, reviewed them and changed the amounts to fit the overall funds. ECA reserved the right of continuous review with subsequent adjustments. This resulted in: 1) the refusal of ECA to allow certain dollar payments in the British balance of payments; 2) Suspension of the Indonesian program entirely; 3) Noted lag in shipment of certain raw materials. These resulted in no drastic changes. France, with very bad inflation, was given aid on condition that it would control inflation after July 1948. This program of self-discipline by the OEEC proved to be a particularly useful tactic, for countries accepted regulation more willingly when imposed by their own unit than if the decision was made by an outside agency. The logic of the whole Program also must have had some convincing merit for the procedure was designed to lead to normal trade relations, with some sacrifice, to be sure, but an understandable one that evidently was desirable. The problems of maintaining a sound monetary system, of working out a plan to handle trade balances, and the need for less discrimination between the products of their neighbors had to be faced and solutions advanced and these were taken in their stride by OEEC.

West Germany's Status

As we have already noted, the three West Zones of Germany participated in the Organization for European Economic Cooperation under the control and guidance of the military governors. General Lucius D. Clay and General Brian H. Robertson of the American and British Zones respectively were men of unusual ability and deeply conscious of their responsibility to the German people and their future. Neither of them were in the original Paris Conference of the CEEC, nor were they represented in it, but later as the ECA was being set up they were consulted as to the participation of their Zones, and they both agreed that the combined Bizonal Economic Council should be the operating unit for the two zones, and this eventually was the arrangement agreed upon.

In June 1947, after Secretary Marshall's speech proposing a cooperative approach to the economic problem, which had been growing worse for some time, a Congressional Committee visited Germany and the Germans were encouraged to believe that they should be included in the proposed plan [5]). Later, after Communist efforts to discourage German participation failed, Bizonia was invited to become a member of OEEC with General Robertson in charge and a group of German technicians from the Bizonal organization. This was the first opportunity for the Germans, even indirectly, to participate in an international undertaking after the war. The original proposal of OEEC was that all funds provided for Germany would be on a loan basis with no grants whatsoever. Moreover, counterpart funds were to be entirely at the disposal of the ECA Administrator. The first allocation of ECA funds was only $ 364,000,000, much smaller than those of some countries with far smaller populations. It was apparent that the feelings of the European countries blinded them to the fact that they could not recover without Germany. The Bizonal unit had requested $ 500,000,000, and after subsequent argument the amount agreed on was $ 414,000,000.

The problem of representation was also in controversy. ECA wanted a German representative from each Zone, but General Clay refused such an arrangement, and after much argument it was agreed that W. Averill Harriman should be the representative with a deputy located in Frankfurt. With the establishment of the Federal Republic of Germany in 1949, the new government set up a special cabinet minister for the Marshall Plan funds with rank as deputy Chancellor. With the transfer of power from Military Government, the Federal Republic became a full-fledged member of the OEEC.

The situation in Germany, after the armistice in May 1945, was naturally very different from that of other European countries. There was no German Government as such and the affairs of occupation were supposed to be conducted by the Allied Control Council, composed of the four Military Governors. We have already noted the fact that the Soviet refusal to operate under the Yalta and Potsdam Agreements, which planned to have the affairs of Germany handled as one unit and when cooperative administration became impossible, because of Soviet refusal to operate on that basis, it was necessary for each of the Western Zone governors to take over. This frustration delayed the possibility for rehabilitation in Germany. The occupying powers had no choice but to provide for the physical needs of the German people. Food had to be brought in in large quantities, as well as medical supplies and other necessities.

GARIOA — Army Aid

Under a program called Government Aid and Relief to Occupied Areas, Congress voted funds to be used by the American Army to meet the urgent needs of the population. In 1945 to 1948, $ 1,010,000,000 was channeled through this organization [6]). When the West German Government became a regular participant in the OEEC, the unused portions of that fund were transferred to the ECA allotment. Counterpart funds under GARIOA had been paid directly to the United States Army blocked accounts which could be used only with the consent of the U.S. Military Governor and later the ECA Administrator. Yet, while this limitation may have seemed a disadvantage, it resulted in a policy of prudent investment of capital funds in industry with the accumulation of interest and amortization which built up the principal amount steadily and gave Germany a much needed pool of investment funds.

Even after the European Recovery Act was passed by Congress and signed by the President, the opponents of foreign aid continued to fight it. Senators Taft, Capehart, Malone and others battled steadily to reduce the amount of the aid if they could not defeat the measure itself. On one of these occasions, Senator Arthur Vandenberg stated in reply: "In spite of comments to the contrary, European nations are not up to pre-war levels because their production has not come up to that point, for they have lost: 1) their income from investments abroad; 2) their income from shipping through loss of ships; and 3) their income from tourist trade. These loomed very large in their national incomes. Furthermore, population has increased through forced migrations. Recovery should not be halfway" [7]).

The first year's ECA funds were used largely for food by Germany because the situation was still desperate. The average daily caloric ration in all three zones was below normal but in the French Zone it approached 1,000 per day which is dangerously low. No workman can do a good

25

day's work on that caloric intake. The German school children were given a good meal at noon to provide enough for their needs. Since the separation of East Germany, Germany itself could not produce enough food for the people and imports were absolutely necessary. Naturally this fundamental human need was given first priority. Housing was also a serious need but it had to wait, as did clothing, and less elemental needs. Repairs to water systems, sewers, electric power plants, and transportation had to be among the first to get attention. Fortunately, General Clay, with a background of engineering training, recognized these facts and under his direction substantial progress was made from the beginning of his administration as Military Governor.

[1] p. 60, American Resources, New York Times, 19 Oct. 1947.
[2] Impact of Foreign Aid Program on Domestic Economy, New York Times, 2 Nov. 1947.
[3] Economic Aid to Europe, Compiled by Robert E. Summers, U.S. Government Report, 1948.
[4] cf. p. 57, First Report on European Recovery Program and U.S. Aid 30 June 1948 Economic Cooperation Administration.
[5] p. 215 ff., Lucius D. Clay, Decision in Germany, New York, Doubleday, 1950.
[6] p. 16—17, 80th Congress, 2nd Session, January to December 1948, Vol. 94, Part I, Table 2, Net Foreign Aid Furnished to European Recovery by countries, July 1948 through June 30, 1951.
[7] p. 3175, 81st Congress, First Session, January to October 1949, Vol. 95, Part I.

Chapter III

PROGRESS IN THE FIRST YEAR — APRIL, 1948 - JUNE, 1949

Initiating the European Recovery Program

The first year (or really 15 months since it started in early April, 1948 and ran to 30 June 1949, the end of the U.S. fiscal year) of the Marshall Plan Program as the European Recovery Program came to be called, was spectacularly successful. Although Germany had not made much progress previously for various reasons, other European countries had made considerable advance in their export program. They had accomplished some rehabilitation, but in early 1948 they were in a slump and there was "austerity" everywhere. To provide funds for foreign exchange, all nations were trying to cut down imports and holding their own populations down to parsimonious rations. For instance, Denmark, a well-known producer of dairy products, was withholding most of them for foreign export. These stringent regulations were a severe handicap in rebuilding a country and most of them desperately needed to do just that. The sudden release of restrictions following the availability of ECA funds naturally brought a boom in consumer supplies as well as the essentials of production.

The European Recovery bill that passed Congress in April, 1948, specified three objectives: 1) "the promoting of industrial, agricultural and cultural production in participating countries; 2) furthering the restoration and maintenance of the soundness of European currencies, budgets, and finances; and 3) facilitating and stimulating the growth of international trade of the participating countries with one another and with other countries by appropriate measures, including the reduction of barriers which hamper trade". Congress further specified that ECA was to finance only that portion of the foreign trade for which dollars must be paid out, but were unavailable from the countries' own resources or from other resources such as the International Bank for Reconstruction and Development. It was expected that during the first year, ECA would finance only about one-half of its dollar imports and these were only about 5 % of the total. The remaining 95 % would be produced or imported through the nation's own resources.

We should probably remind ourselves that the European Recovery Program was planned to cover four years only. While a total amount of probable spending for aid was discussed, it was agreed in the Congress that appropriations would be made for one year at a time and the Program would be reviewed each year in the light of what had been accomplished and what was urgently needed. The final date set for the Program was 30 June 1952. ECA knew well that much of the early expenditure would have to be for food and medical supplies but it was primarily interested in the funding of manufacture so that industries would become independent of continuing aid. This, of course, meant securing machine tools and equipment, raw materials, trained labor, and improved management. In the field of agriculture there was the need of better seeds, fertilizers, machinery, and modern methods. The shortage of skilled manpower and modern technical methods were handicaps to industry that would need to be corrected. It was hoped that the counterpart funds would be used for such improvements. Not the least among the urgent requirements were the steps to be taken to balance national budgets and to maintain a stable currency.

One of the problems faced by the United States was the protection of the American economy only now recovering from a war program, and with the inflated consumer demand running considerable risk of inflation of some proportions. The United States had to restrict exports on those commodities that were in short supply, such as foods, — eggs, wool, tung oil, hemp fibres, turpentine and seeds. Maximum use of private trade channels was to be encouraged. Price levels were to be maintained without undue increases. Private relief shipments and travel were to be stimulated. In retrospect the risks do not seem great but for those who were responsible for the economic progress and stability of the United States, this recovery program funding was a project that had its dangers as well as its possibilities for success. Perhaps its main risk was the question of changing the depressed attitude of most Europeans as to their future.

The First Quarter — 9 April to 30 June 1948

The ECA financed Supply Program used existing private channels of purchasing such as: Individuals and concerns, associations of European business men, foreign government purchasing agencies and U.S. Government procurement agencies. The total funds allotted for the first stage of ERP was $ 5,055,000,000 [1]). The $ 55,000,000 was for the use of the State Department to complete its final operations under the U.S. Foreign Aid Program. The amount of funds for the first quarter, 9 April to 30 June, 1948 was $ 1,371,300,000, 80 % in grants and 20 % in loans. By the end of that first quarter goods and services amounting to $ 1,086,000,000 were scheduled for delivery and much was already in Europe. The distribution of this supply program was: Food, feed foods, and fertilizers — 33 %; Fuel — 20 %; Raw and semi-finished products — 22 %; Machinery and equipment — 7 %; other products — 3 %; and ocean freight — 15 %. The sources of the commodities were: the United States — 57 %; Canada and Newfoundland — 21 %; Latin America — 6 %; participating countries — 10 %; Other — 6 %. The total supply program for this quarter was: $ 1,316,300,000; with typical grants: Britain — $ 400,000,000; France — $ 335,000,000; Italy — $ 158,000,000; West Germany — $ 120,000,000; Netherlands — $ 105,000,000, and other lesser amounts. The European Recovery Program was off to a good start and the most immediate result beyond the availability of goods, was the changed attitude of Europeans working in the cooperative program of the sixteen countries and Germany.

In the fifteen months of operations, ECA actually authorized the purchase of $ 5,419,999,999 worth of commodities, of which 67 % came from the United States. During the second quarter of 1949 — April, May and June — 100 % of the bread grains, coarse grains, dairy products, cotton, tobacco, motor vehicles, and aircraft for which authorizations were issued came from the United States; likewise, 95 % of the fats and oils, chemical products, and machinery and equipment; and 85 % of the iron and steel mill products and lumber came from the United States. The actual figures on Supply Sources show that the United States was supplying 2/3 of goods authorized. 72 % of the agricultural products and 63 % of the industrial goods came from the United States in this period [2]).

With this general summary, let us note briefly the progress in the five quarters of the first year, from April, 1948 to 30 June, 1949. The first quarter saw the beginning of the Program, but in spite of the problem of securing staff members and setting up organization, the progress was excellent. The ECA and OEEC had determined that $ 1,371,300,000 be allotted to the first quarter.

The Second Quarter — 1 July to 30 September 1948

The allotments for the second quarter — totaled $ 1,930,300,000, with major allocations to: Britain — $ 447,900,000; France — $ 473,500,000; West Germany — $ 260,300,000; Italy — $ 257,900,000; Netherlands — $ 172,800,000 and other smaller amounts to the remaining countries. By this time the Organization for European Economic Cooperation had become a smoothly working agency. The Council of member nations was vested with power of decision and it could act without endless parliamentary discussion. The Secretariat, composed of the Secretary General and his staff along with technical committees prepared questionnaires and instructions to study and reconcile the replies from the participating nations. The various committees concerned themselves with special problems, with liaison with other European agencies, and with the world market situations. The resulting uniform pattern for all nations produced an effective and equitable operating agency that was of immense value in the whole Program. It handled not only the determination of needs and allocations of goods but it had developed the intra-European trade and payments plan to handle multilateral balances. This Convention was signed in Paris, 16 October 1948 and became a very effective means of stimulating trade. Special problems of machinery and capital equipment needs were studied continually in the light of past national performance and future market opportunities. It was a diplomatic problem of high order to adjust the aid to the hopes and ambitions of each of the participating nations. The Program was proving its effectiveness in the promotion of agricultural production, by increasing the use of commercial fertilizers such as nitrogen, phosphorus and potash. The introduction of hybrid corn seed produced greater fodder, and the wider production of farm machinery in France, United Kingdom, Italy, Belgium and Bizone of Germany was developed to supplement the Congressional limit of exports of this item from the United States to $ 75,000,000. The 30 % increase in food production in 1948 along with the freer trade between participating countries had gone far in relieving the restrictions in rationing.

The major stimulus to industrial recovery in Europe came from the expansion of cooperative action in dealing with the coal and steel industries. The Coal Committee discovered that 1,000,000 metric tons of coal was stored and not moving into production. Better mining, better transportation and better use of varieties of coal were developed for those countries in which they were needed. The improvement of inland transportation was an important development. The rehabilitation of railroads made it possible to reinstate the pre-war exchange through the efforts of OEEC. The International Railways Union undertook to work out a standardization of rolling stock so that repair practices could be improved. It was pointed out that if ocean shipping could be partially diverted to use Rotterdam and Antwerp and then the Rhine barges, more than 8,000 freight cars could be released for other services.

The restoration and maintenance of monetary stability was one of the major conditions prerequisite to European economic recovery. The expansion of industrial production had to rest upon a normal trade between nations. ECA had emphasized this fact and encouraged such international trade not only between participating countries but also with other nations. On 7 August 1948, the OEEC issued the following statement: "Unless internal equilibrium is re-established within the various participating countries, increased production, whether in Europe or elsewhere, will not enable participating countries to balance their external accounts either with the rest of the world as a whole or with the dollar area. The internal price structure must be such as to encourage, not discourage exports, in particular exports to the dollar area; the internal monetary policy must be such as to encourage and make possible the necessary volume of saving in both the public and private sphere which can make possible the investment program.

"Unless general policies are adopted which will establish internal equilibrium in various participating countries, increased production will not enable them to balance accounts. The responsibility rests upon each country. Outside aid cannot be effective unless adequate measures are taken to meet internal difficulties." [3])

Third Quarter — 1 October to 31 December 1948

There was excellent progress during the third period of the European Recovery Program primarily due to favorable harvests and the increased supply of raw materials through the ECA. The participating countries had been able to avoid economic collapse and to advance in the recovery program. Table below shows the Industrial Production Indexes from 1946 to 1948 for a group of the participating countries. While the index number for West Germany improved slightly through this period it was still behind the other countries and naturally pulled down the average for the other countries. Even the fourth quarter index number 64, was still far below any other index number. Because of Germany's key position in Western Europe it reduced the progress of other countries.

Industrial Production Indexes, 1946—48 [4])
(1938 — 100)

Country	1946	1947	1948
Total:			
Including Western Germany	76	87	99
Excluding Western Germany	90	103	114
Belgium	88	106	116
Denmark	101	116	129
France	79	95	108
Greece	57	71	77
Ireland	110	116	132
Italy	58	76	81
Netherlands	74	94	112
Norway	100	115	125
Sweden	135	138	143
United Kingdom	102	110	123
Western Germany	29	34	51

A strike of French miners cut coal production 5,500,000 metric tons and prevented reaching the OEEC goal for the period but increased production in Bizone raised the quarter production 4 % above 1947 but it was still 16 % below the pre-war average. By the end of this period, 30 December 1948, the total procurement authorizations had totaled $ 4,044,800,000, including $ 3,707,000,000 for commodities, $ 336,700,000 for ocean freight and $ 1,200,000 for technical services. The United Kingdom, with approved procurements of $ 645,500,000 was the chief beneficiary as usual. This country along with France and Italy accounted for about 2/3 of all the authorizations issued. Ireland, Sweden and Turkey who had not received any aid previously, received their first authorizations. By the end of the first nine months of ECA the United Kingdom and France had accounted for 51 % of all authorizations; Italy, the Netherlands, and the Bizone of Germany for another 30 %, with the remaining countries and the French Zone receiving nineteen per cent [5]).

The Fourth Quarter — 1 January to 31 March 1949

Progress continued during the fourth quarter during which most countries participating in the ECA reached pre-war levels, averaged almost 1/7 above that mark. This was a gain of 15 % from the last quarter, resulting largely from the increased output of the laborer and the steady flow of raw materials. Inflation appeared to be practically halted at this time. Earnings of the ERP countries paid almost 2/3 of their imports in 1948 compared with less than 1/2 in 1947. The deficit remaining amounted to $ 5,600,000,000 chiefly in dollars. To close the gap, exports would have to be greatly expanded by 1952 through multilateral trade.

It is interesting to note that during the first six months of operation of the payments plan, it had definitely promoted trade between the participating countries. Cooperative investment plans were being developed to increase power supply and there had been impressive increase in land transportation. Advances had been made in lifting restrictions on travel and inducements had been developed to facilitate the transfer of manpower to areas of demand for labor. We should note that deposits made in special counterpart funds at this time amounted to the equivalent of $ 1,733,200,000. Approvals for program use by the various countries amounted to $ 1,318,400,000 of the 95 % of deposits of $ 1,646,600,000. The amount reserved for use by the United States, 5 %, was $ 86,000,000. The Intra-European payment plan handled $ 67,700,000 during this period compared with $ 30,900,000 for the previous quarter. Belgium and the Netherlands had worked out a plan for a customs union to develop greater volume of trade between them; France and Italy had signed an agreement for a customs union; and the Scandinavian countries set up a similar arrangement. OEEC and ECA had encouraged this effort. By the end of this period, procurement authorizations [6]) totaled $ 4,891,700,000, of which the United Kingdom received $ 1,315,500,000, France received $ 1,084,800,000, Italy $ 582,100,000, Netherlands $ 471,400,000 and Bizone of Germany $ 384,500,000.

The Fifth Quarter — 1 April to 30 June 1949

The fifth or final quarter of the first year, ending with the U.S. Government fiscal year at 30 June 1949 brought another stage of success. The index of production for Europe reached a point 18 % above the pre-war 1938 level, with record output for steel, coal, textile yarn, cement and motor vehicles. Inability to reduce the dollar gap continued to be the major problem for Europe. Exports to the United States from ERP countries declined in volume. There was reduced export in the first two quarters of 1949 in structural steel, aluminum, automobiles, tractors, iron and steel scrap, old brass and clippings and pig iron which accounted for a drop of $ 29,600,000 in this period. Technical assistance had been increasing and in this period amounted to $ 2,466,025. This program had brought American experts to ERP countries as consultants to industries, and had also taken European business men and technicians to the United States for training. The import trade with the United States continued to dominate the ECA program with 72 % of the agricultural supplies and 63 % of the industrial commodities coming from American sources.

Germany's Limitations

In this discussion, we have dealt with the general advance in Europe and have spent little time on the progress in Germany. There are two reasons for this seeming over-sight: 1) Germany was still under the occupation control of the three Military Governments and although it had experienced a currency change that laid a foundation for economic progress it was in no condition to begin that effort. 2) Although the Bizone was the beneficiary of the GARIOA Fund and some progress had been made in 1946—1948, received relatively small amounts in loans only, during the first periods, were granted and those called conditional grants. The total amount of Marshall Plan assistance received by the Bizone of Germany during this period was $ 613,500,000, of which $ 478,000,000 was ECA aid and the remainder was from the GARIOA Fund administered by the United States Army. On 30 June 1949 the Bizone of Germany had paid into the Special Counterpart accounts the amount of $ 214,600,000 and the French Zone had paid $ 62,500,000. These were dollar equivalents of the Deutsch Marks and Francs. None of the French fund had been approved for withdrawal and only $ 1,200,000 had been withdrawn after approval from the Bizone account.

The German technicians and economists who worked with the occupation officers at Paris and in Germany were making valuable contributions and getting acquainted with the problems. It may be said that in this period the German units were distinctly second class participants completely under the control of the Military regime. It was not until the establishment of the Federal Republic that the West Germans came into their own as actual participants completely free from control of the Military regime and actual participants in the ECA and its functions.

Currency Change

The first quarter of West Germany's participation in the Marshall Plan Program was especially significant. On 15 June 1948, the West Zones undertook a currency change that eliminated the old depreciated Reichsmark and brought in the new Deutsche Mark with adequate financial backing. The exchange was really drastic allowing only 6½ of the new Deutsche Marks for each 100 of the old Reichsmarks. The 6 were for free use and the ½ for blocked accounts or medium and long term credits. Some accumulations were wiped out entirely, for instance, the blocked amount of the American film producers. This group had been exceedingly generous in supplying film for use in German cinemas, the fees for which had to be placed in block accounts from which they could not be withdrawn. When the currency conversion came, the entire accumulation was wiped out. It is to their credit that they did not refuse to continue their generous policy. Of course, black market operators were caught by the exchange but they usually counted on barter not money in their transaction. The psychological reaction to the conversion was stoical, — as if it had been expected. Once it had taken place, people shook off their losses and looked ahead to savings which could be trusted. It was true that many of the older business men had experienced deflation twice before and they looked upon it as a cathartic from which business would react positively and the economic system could build constructively. With a sound currency, it was expected that Germany could begin its recovery with confidence. Without this change there could have been no real improvement in the economy for the whole system rested upon a sound currency.

The Dismantling Problem

Another major development occurred in this period that was crucial in turning the attitude of Germans toward the future. Before the signing of the armistice, it had been decided by the Allies that the reparations demanded after World War I had been the major cause of the economic disaster which followed, therefore, there would be no reparations payments, but those who had won the war were not to be denied entirely. It was finally agreed that where an idustrial plant in Allied countries had been destroyed during the war and the nation which lost it could find a similar plant in Germany to replace it, that plant could be dismantled and taken away. While there was some orderly procedure, much of the operation was slipshod and did not always prove a claim to such an item. Nor did the Allied Governments seem to give thought to the fact that every industrial plant in Germany had been used hard and was in poor condition so that the claimant might well be getting something that was not far from junk. Yet, every time a plant was released for dismantling the town or city residents saw their jobs and livelihood being taken away.

Mr. Paul Hoffman, ECA Administrator, immediately saw that if the dismantling program was continued that Germany would never know what to plan for the future, nor could newly equipped plants be protected from claims. When he brought the matter up with the OEEC, there was reluctance to take any action, the bitterness of the war was still in the minds of national leaders. So in characteristic directness he went to President Truman, explained the situation, and asked that some immediate action be taken to avoid further delay and trouble. After consultation with the Allied nations, it was agreed that a special committee should be appointed, chiefly of American business leaders and technical experts to examine each of the cases, to make inspections and recommend action. 914 plants, or parts thereof, were listed for dismantling in the three West Zones at that time. After consultations, all but 381 were dropped and this number were carefully inspected and recommendations made that all be kept in Germany. The result was another psychological lift for the German people [7]).

The European Payments Union (EPU)

A third problem arose as soon as trade between nations began in volume, namely, the limitations of bilateral treaties for international trade. It was literally impossible to balance imports and exports between any two countries. Only when the total trade was considered was there any satisfactory balance. It might take three or half a dozen international import-export operations to balance out the difference resulting. The OEEC again studied this problem and proposed a practical multilateral compensations system which eventually took the form of a European Payments Union, which could serve as a clearing unit for all international trade of the participating nations and arrive at a balance of the total. Arrangements were made with the Bank of International Settlements at Basle, Switzerland to act as the clearing agent for OEEC. Since all European currencies were not convertible, the B.I.S. had to get the consent of the creditor to use a so-called "secondary category compensation" for temporary adjustment. When major credits and debits developed these were paid off either by the B.I.S or the debtor in dollars or gold. Minor changes were necessary from time to time but this system operated effectively during the remainder of the Program [8]). For one thing, the participating countries learned how to work together in a sound and practical program of recovery in which they came to consider themselves as partners not competitors. They learned the values of multilateral trade between members of a group over a bilateral arrangement. They had developed a balance of payments plan which stimulated trade and eliminated much of the transfer of dollars or gold. They had built new plants with modern machinery and they were prepared to enter world markets. Europe was by no means entirely recovered, and much remained to be done in the ensuing years of the ERP, but it was making progress.

[1] cf. Ch. II, First Report to Congress, Economic Cooperation Administration, 9 April to 30 June, 1948. U.S. Government Printing Office.

[2] p. 55, Fifth Report to Congress, Economic Cooperation Administration, 1 April to 30 June, 1949, U. S. Government Printing Office.

[3] cf. p. 17, Second Report of the Economic Cooperation Administration, 1 July to 30 September 1948, U. S. Government Printing Office.

[4] Adapted from Table B-1, p. 126, Third Report to Congress, Economic Cooperation Administration, Quarter ending 31 December 1948, U. S. Government Printing Office.

[5] p. 134, Third Report to Congress, Economic Cooperation Administration, Quarter ending 31 December 1948, U. S. Government Printing Office.

[6] cf p. 104—5, Fourth Report to Congress, Economic Cooperation Administration, Period from 1 January to 31 March 1949, U. S. Government Printing Office.

[7] cf. p. 48, Third Report to Congress by the Economic Cooperation Administration, Quarter ending 31 Dec. 1948, U. S. Government Printing Office.

[8] cf. p. 14 ff., Second Report to Congress, Economic Cooperation Administration, 1 July to 30 September 1948, U. S. Government Printing Office.

Chapter IV

PROGRESS DURING THE SECOND YEAR OF
THE EUROPEAN RECOVERY PROGRAM

Anticipating the Future

With the beginning of the new fiscal year 1 July 1949 — 30 June 1950 in the United States and the projecting of the program for the coming four quarters, the OEEC outlined a course of action for itself with definite objectives for the remaining years aside from the matter of aid and supply. A consultative group consisting of the Foreign Ministers of seven participating countries assisted in the discussion and elaboration of the following eight principles for carrying out the proposals. On 26 March, the nineteen member Council of OEEC approved the plan of action.

1) *"On the national level, 1949 must be a year of financial and monetary stabilization in Europe.* It is proposed that each member nation should send to the OEEC a report on its internal financial position, showing the difficulties it has faced in the past few years, the methods adopted to meet them, the results achieved, and finally the steps proposed to attain or maintain monetary stability during 1949.

2) *"A rapid increase in exports is an essential condition for the success of the European Recovery Program. Of equal importance with the development of exports is the increase of invisible earnings and in particular from tourism and shipping.* Each member country was asked to submit to the OEEC as soon as possible a report on special steps it is taking to ensure the success, of its export drive, especially in the dollar area, to reduce or eliminate trade barriers, and to initiate other measures designed to implement this principle. The Executive Committee of OEEC was requested forthwith to arrange for a preliminary examination of each country's estimate of export earnings, and to determine whether a definite system of exchanging information or techniques of conducting export drives and other steps might be taken to increase exports, especially to the dollar area. The Committee was also requested to provide for investigation of costs of production and prices in the participating coun-

tries, particularly with a view to determining what effect the reduction of costs and prices might have in expanding exports to and reducing imports from the dollar area. The Committee was also called upon to launch a study of the countries' estimates of invisible earnings (from tourist travel, shipping and emigrant remittances) and examine the measures that might be taken jointly to ensure the maximum payable benefits from these sources of income.

3) *"The danger to the economy of Western Europe from a drastic and sudden reduction of imports when the European Recovery Program ends must be forestalled by a continual re-examination of current import programs, particularly so as to curtail dollar imports not vitally needed in order to establish the necessary balance between imports payable in dollars and available resources.* Each country was asked to reduce its imports from the dollar area to the extent necessary to eliminate by 1952—53 the need for extraordinary outside assistance after taking into account all available dollar sources. In doing so, every effort should be made to secure an acceptable standard of living and a high level of economic activity. The reduction of dollar imports should so far as possible involve commodities available from non-dollar sources, and every effort should be made to expand world trade and develop, in cooperation with other countries, new sources of supply in the participating nations, their dependent overseas territories and other areas. In carrying out these measures, the ultimate objective should be the re-establishment of multilateral trade on an expanding basis.

"If supply difficulties should persist for products essential to the maintenance or development of economic activity, the OEEC will study ways of remedying these difficulties, either through existing international allocation schemes or by other means.

"The countries should make progress each year toward elimination of the need for extraordinary outside assistance but should not plan on the assumption that they can earn gold or dollars from each other. Special attention should be given to certain types of commodities in view of their importance to the European economy (for example, foodstuffs and feeds, coal, and petroleum) or because of persistent scarcity, as in non-ferrous metals.

4) *"Steps must be taken towards the elimination of internal disequilibrium in Europe, this process to be assisted by an adequate system of intra-European payments leading to a healthy expansion of trade between participating countries.*

"The Executive Committee of the OEEC was asked to take the necessary steps to obtain a full report on the extent to which the respite given by the intra-European payment plan of 1948—49 had corrected the inbalance in intra-European trade and had promoted a healthy expansion of multilateral commerce among the participating countries. The nations were invited to discuss with each other their trade exchanges and other elements of their balance of payments for 1949—50 and inform the Executive Committee of the estimated deficits. The Trade and Payments Committee were to examine the results of these discussions as well as the measures to be taken to achieve further progress in reducing or eliminating trade barriers and furthering multilateral commerce.

5) *"Investment and modernization projects should be developed rationally and in concert along the following lines: a) by taking care to avoid creating a production capacity in excess of resources; b) by concentration on the projects most likely to improve Europe's balance of payments with the outside world and more particularly to result in a speedy reduction of the dollar deficit and c) by attaching special importance to investments in overseas territories.*

6) *"A system should be devised by which participating countries can coordinate investments and exchange information needed for common decisions.*

"The proposals under Principles 5 and 6 directed the Executive Committee to initiate a study of the national investment programs and draw up a list of industries which might be considered suitable for coordination among the participating countries. The Committee was requested to see that appropriate publicity is given by the governments, bearing in mind the market possibilities expected if multilateral world trade expands. The investment programs should be reviewed with special attention to the development in dependent overseas territories of materials that are, or may be expected to be, in short supply.

7) *"A start should be made in the problem of surplus population in certain parts of Europe.* The Executive Committee was directed to obtain and present to the OEEC council a detailed report containing practical and precise proposals for solving this problem and also to see that due consideration was given the manpower question in examining the production, trade and investment problems involved in recovery.

8) *"The Council hereby decides to review, at regular intervals, progress toward the above objectives.* This survey will be based on periodic reports to be submitted by participating countries to the organization." [1]) This program for the anticipated ending of the ECA or Marshall Plan Aid indicated the degree of cooperation which had grown up among the participating nations. The end of aid in 1952 would certainly produce radical changes in economic activities unless some constructive steps were taken. It was a wise policy to anticipate what would have to be done by 1952. The results of this preliminary exploratory plan were evident in later years.

Devaluation in Britain and its Consequences

The unsteady economic conditions in the July-August-September period had come to the place where some steps had to be taken. From 1946 to 1949 exports had steadily increased from $ 3,000,000,000 to $ 6,000,000,000. The increase had held up until the second quarter of 1949 and then there was a sharp reverse. Trade with dollar areas declined and trade barriers appeared. Studies by OEEC showed that by the middle of 1949 European currencies were over-valued from 15 to 40 %. Moreover, hard currency reserves were low. Gold and dollar reserves declined to $ 1,400,000,000 from $ 1,600,000,000 in March 1949. Too much of the British trade had been with countries whose currencies were soft and there was no help from that source. In the Spring, industrial production had increased to 37 % above the pre-war level and exports had been high to the United States. Then they fell off and the weakness of the sterling area was evident along with inflationary pressures. Greater exports to the countries with soft currency continued and prices of British goods were higher than those in the United States. OEEC and ECA consulted frequently with British authorities and finally on September 16, 1949 the

United Kingdom announced a currency devaluation from $ 4.03 to $ 2.80 for the pound in relation to American dollar. This was approved by the International Monetary Fund and announced on September 18, 1949. It was a 30.5 % devaluation and took most of Europe and Latin America with it. All the sterling area nations, Norway, Iceland, Sweden, Denmark, the Netherlands, Austria, Finland, Egypt, and Jordan reduced the same amount. France and Italy who had repeatedly lowered their exchange rates devalued another 5 and 9 % to the dollar. West Germany, already severely devalued in 1948 devalued another 21 %. Uruguay and the Argentine kept their exchange rates but revised rates applying to particular transaction of imports and exports. Greece and Israel followed England's devaluation; Canada reduced 10 %. No change was made by Switzerland, Pakistan, Brazil and the Eastern European countries, other Latin American countries and the Near East. The United States made no change.

This pattern of devaluation meant that a radical adjustment occurred in the prices of imports from dollar areas. It took 44 % more to buy the same quantity of goods in countries that devalued 30.5 %. The cost of merchandise to dollar countries was proportionately lower. Most prices had been stabilized; some in ERP countries dropped. Many prices on large bulk shipments were revised slowly.

Although the effects of devaluation were not immediately evident, Europe did take the shock without difficulty because it had already achieved some stability through OEEC's collaboration in the process. Stability in the United States was not disturbed. World demand for food was strong and soft currencies were raised; the hard currencies were not lowered. Nevertheless, the cost of living did increase. United Kingdom regulations required that pre-devaluation stocks should be sold at those prices. Some set multiple prices with one for national and another for international purchases. Unfortunately, devaluation diverted more exports to soft currency. This whole matter might have been a dangerous economic episode, but the participating countries managed to go through it without serious difficulty. With the index for 1938 as the base, 100, the changes for all Europe were 103 and 101 for the 2 nd and 3rd quarters in 1948; 117 for both quarters in 1949.

The First Quarter — 1 July to 30 September 1949

The Bizone index for the same periods were: 43 and 56 for 1948; and 75 and 77 for 1949, with increases of 70 % and 37 %. The Bizone industrial production continued to expand especially in the consumer goods field. Two world wars, a world depression and the persistence of foreign exchange problems had produced protectionist and nationalist measures. The result had been too much compartmentalism of Europe with stifled economic growth. A radical improvement in Europe's position in world markets without impairing its standard of living depended, to a large extent, on the creation of a wide area of free trade where mass production and intensive competition could be restored. It was recognized that the best solution was an integrated economy in Western Europe without restriction on the movement of goods and without monetary barriers and tariffs. Through the end of September, $ 7,086,000,000 had been allotted to the participating countries by ECA; $ 5,953,000,000 during the first 15 months of operations and $ 1,133,000,000 more in the July to September quarter of 1949/50. Industrial projects in participating countries costing $ 264,000,000 of ECA funds was about 20 % of the expected total cost. Nearly 3/4 of the ECA funds were earmarked for modernization or expansion. It is interesting to note that ECA funds did not pay all the cost of this improvement but it did provide the incentive that brought about such industrial advances.

Counterpart Funds

During this quarter ECA approved projects for the withdrawal of the counterpart funds under Public Law 472 for the amount equivalent to $ 770,000,000, making the total approved amount since the beginning of the ERP program the equivalent of $ 2,639,000,000, 56 % of these special funds were used for expansion of productive enterprises. The United Kingdom had used most of its counterpart funds for the retirement of debt as an inflationary measure. The equivalent of $ 739,000,000 had been applied to this use.

Western Germany had not had counterpart funds released to it until September 1949. ECA agreed to the first major use of counterpart funds in Germany as a capital investment loans to operators of Ruhr coal mines. The funds were made available through the Reconstruction Loan Corporation in Germany. This was a part of the program to provide equipment for substantial increases of coal production, 44,000,000 DM were allotted to the completion of a new power station in the western sectors of Berlin to make this area independent of the Soviet sector electric power and also saving 175,000 tons of coal annually through more efficient operations. ECA also approved the use of 57,000,000 DM in the French zone for railway reconstruction. A portion of these funds were subsequently used to pay German exporters for drawing rights extended through the intra-European payments plan. Such withdrawals amounted to $ 321,000,000 DM.

The Second Quarter — 1 October to 31 December 1949

The second quarter of the current year showed further progress in the ERP. With renewed stability following the devaluation of many currencies after Britain's devaluation of 30.5 % economic affairs took on a more normal posture. Procurements authorized during this quarter amounted to $ 1,046,000,000, with the United Kingdom getting $ 329,500,000; France $ 191,800,000, the Federal Republic of Germany $ 104,800,000; Italy $ 104,700,000 and the Netherlands $ 69,600,000.

Balance of Trade

The persistent problem of balancing Europe's dollar account was not easily solved. It was recognized that as Europe's exports to America increased, imports might be increased, but in the past 30 years the United States had steadily become less dependent on Europe. During the period from 1900 to 1913, imports averaged per year about 2 % of all American imports; in 1949—50 it was hardly 1/3 of one per cent. This drop indicated that European manufacturers lacked the flexibility in marketing and development to meet demands of the American trade. The OEEC recommended a restudy of what the United States would buy so as to produce goods for American customers. Part of the difficulty had been the restrictive trade practices in Europe with cartels and tariffs and quotas to protect manufacturers from competitive imports. The OEEC undertook to study the removal of trade barriers as the next step beyond multilateral balances which were handled by the European Payments Union.

Industrial Production

Industrial production for this period was up to an average of 120, well above the pre-war figure. Agricultural production was up 5 % from the 1948—49 level and 3 % above the pre-war level. Food consumption had reached 2,800 calories a day compared with 2,765 for 1948 and 2,900 before the war. The American average was 3,240. The increased intra-European trade was about 97 % of the 1938 level. The European payments plan had cleared an equivalent of $ 45,000,000 in this quarter, the largest volume to that date. There was a small rise in the cost of living but wholesale prices had been steady following devaluation. The output per man in this period was higher than 1938 in France, Ireland, Sweden, Switzerland, Turkey and the United Kingdom; it was about the same in Belgium, Denmark, Greece, Norway; it was moderately lower in the Netherlands, and considerably lower in Austria, Italy and West Germany. The total allotments under the ECA program amounted to $ 8,527,000,000 since April 1948 [2]).

German Aid

West Germany had received $ 848,700,000 to date, of which $ 613,500,000 was allotted since the West German government took over. The GARIOA funds were carried over from the Bizone officers to the Federal Republic. The Counterpart Fund accounts showed a total withdrawal on 31 December 1949 of $ 3,045,000,000, of which Germany's account was the largest, $ 186,000,000 or 779,000,000 DM. 600,000,000 DM of this was earmarked for increasing industrial production and 172,000,000 DM to pay German exporters for goods shipped to other countries under the drawing rights in the European payments plan. Under the current arrangements, Germany was making counterpart fund deposits for both ECA dollar aid grants and the conditional aid. The above named 600,000,000 DM was to be used for an investment program totaling 1,000,000,000 DM; 312,000,000 DM to go into major industries. About 220,000,000 DM was earmarked for power plants. Agricultural projects were to receive 124,000,000 DM. About 95,000,000 DM were to be used to stimulate economic activity in Berlin. Loans to industry were used as a source of long-term credits advanced to industry through banks for ECA projects. Counterpart funds were taking the place of capital for investment which Germany lacked at that time.

Under Public Law 472 Congress had authorized ECA to provide investment guarantees for American companies setting up business in Europe. There was little activity during the previous year and at this time only seven companies applied for such service during this quarter and for relatively small amounts. Technical assistance which was relatively small in 1948 now became a growing feature of the ERP. A total of $ 4,956,000 was used to send 350 American technicians to Europe as consultants, and 481 Europeans to the United States in a range of interests of industrial production, public administration, agriculture, transportation, communication, manpower, market research and tourism.

Mutual Defense Needs

On 6 October 1949 the United States Congress enacted the Mutual Defense Assistance Program (Public Law 320, 81st Congress). It was aimed to coordinate the ECA Program with the development of defense and stated that economic recovery should have priority over military aid programs. ECA was represented at Military Defense Assistance Program in an advisory capacity to consider the effect of military programs on the economic systems of the recipient countries, and also the use of ECA allotments and authorizations in furnishing items and commodities similar to those furnished by ECA. The military threat in Europe had brought a new realization of danger, and NATO had been organized to develop an armed screen against aggressive Communism. The problem at this point had become not only how to rehabilitate Western Europe but how to defend it.

Effect on American Economy

A justifiable query may be made in relation to the United States and its progress. The effect of ERP was one of the problems raised by the antagonists of the recovery program. What had happened? In 1946, United States production was high and employment was excellent. In 1949, the United States had a mild recession and emphasis was placed on the use of surplus commodities in the United States for foreign aid. Total exports of goods and services were $ 15,800,000,000 in 1949. $ 1,000,000,000 less than in 1948. ECA paid 16 % to Canada, 9 % to Latin American countries in 1949. Approximately 90 % of ECA funds financed requirements for food and agriculture came from the United States. At the same time, the United States was purchasing strategic materials with some of its share of the counterpart funds. In 1949, $ 5,140,000 included, bauxite from Indonesia, $ 4,500,000, diamonds $ 79,000 from the Netherlands, cryolite $ 525,000 from Denmark. The purchases of these strategic materials in 1949 with approximately one fourth of the counterpart funds available included rubber, sisal, diamonds, bauxite, palm oil, graphite, sperm oil, cryolite, tantalum, beryl and miscellaneous items.

The Federal Republic of Germany becomes a Participating Member of OEEC

Of special interest in this quarter is an entry of the Federal Republic of Germany into the OEEC as a full member and a new agreement with the United States with respect to ECA relations. In the main, this agreement reflected the previous ones signed by the Military Governors in late 1948. The arrangement for payment of counterpart funds was to be the deposit in the Bank Deutscher Länder of marks equivalent to dollars required for purchase of materials, services, and technical information plus the cost of processing, storing, transporting, repairing, etc. This amount was to be computed at the current official rate of exchange unless otherwise agreed. The usual arrangement applied to the 5 % to be reserved for the United States and 95 % to the credit of the paying country to be used for suitable purposes with the approval of ECA. The balance of GARIOA funds was turned over to ECA with such obligations as required from past operations. This consolidation and adjustment of all aid funds was the final change in arrangements and made West Germany fully a member of OEEC. The Adenauer government appointed a cabinet minister to administer the Marshall Plan funds of the Federal Republic in harmony with the provisions of the ECA agreement and the bilateral treaty.

The Third Quarter — 1 January to 31 March 1950
Economic Problems

The predominant characteristic of this period was the decline in over-all United States trade surplus, the lowest since World War II. The dollar gap was a world-wide problem. The reduction of the dollar deficit anywhere helped to relieve the pressure for dollars in the ERP countries. The total commodity trade surplus of the United States during the first calendar quarter declined 60 % compared with the same quarter in 1949; the surplus with Western Europe declined 40 %. Europe's attempt to get prices in line was largely responsible.

U. S. World Trade, by quarters during 1949 and first quarter of 1950 ³)
(figures in millions of dollars)

| Item | 1949 | | | | 1950 |
	1st Qtr.	2nd Qtr.	3rd Qtr.	4th Qtr.	1st Qtr.
Exports	$ 3,325	3,362	2,684	2,629	2,381
Imports	1,790	1,601	1,478	1,759	1,885
U. S. Trade Balance	$ 1,535	1,761	1,206	870	496

At the same time there was an increase in intra-European trade. Payments were better balanced than at any time since the start of the payments plan, 1948. Only a very small portion of deficits required gold payments. OEEC succeeded in getting a new list of commodities imported free; only six nations did not comply with this OEEC effort. West Germany was protecting her manufactured goods but was preparing to establish a free list, and already had such an agreement with Switzerland and Belgium. OEEC hoped to get 75 % of the items on the free list by the end of 1950. The listing of 50 % had not presented any serious problems. Another objective of the OEEC was to reduce restrictive private business practices as a means of stabilizing currency and trade. In this connection, dual pricing was frowned upon. Activity in West Germany increased imports by 25 % over the previous quarter and that meant that it had to draw heavily upon drawing rights assigned to it by the OEEC upon its entry in the previous year.

There was a gain of 9 % in industrial production from the previous first quarter in the previous year. This was largely the result of the United Kingdom's extraordinary rise in industrial production. Sweden's index was the highest but it had been so for some time. Austria showed an 84 % gain and now was up to 127; Norway had 18 % rise and West Germany reaching 82 showed a 100 % gain over 1948.

Index of industrial production [4)]

(1938 — 100)

Country	1948 1st Qtr.	1949 1st Qtr.	1949 4th Qtr.	1950 1st Qtr.	Percentage Change 1st Qtr. '50 from 1st Qtr. '48	1st Qtr. '50 from 1st Qtr. '49
All countries	97	113	120	123	+ 27 %	+ 9 %
Austria	69	95	127	127	+ 84	+ 34
Belgium	112	120	117	116	+ 4	— 3
Denmark	132	138	152	151	+ 14	+ 9
France	110	124	123	121	+ 10	— 2
Germany (Fed. Rep.)	41	70	81	82	+ 100	+ 17
Greece	69	82	99	97	+ 41	+ 18
Ireland	125	132	157	151	+ 21	+ 14
Italy	90	95	107	109	+ 21	+ 15
Netherlands	104	120	139	134	+ 29	+ 12
Norway	125	137	138	147	+ 18	+ 7
Sweden	148	160	165	166	+ 12	+ 4
United Kingdom	128	137	144	149	+ 16	+ 9

Coal production was up 4 % over 1949; the gain in West Germany was 10 %. The shortage of coal was over and shipments from the United States had ceased. France, United Kingdom and Belgium had reduced their quotas. Electric power production had showed more than 100 % gain over 1949 and it was 90 % over the 1938 record. The largest gain was in West Germany, France and Italy. Agriculture production was 3 % above 1949 and just 12 % below 1938. The chief improvement was in meats, which increased 25 %. The total arable land was still 50 % below pre-war. Live stock slaughtered in 1949—50 increased to 64 % of pre-war figure; milk produced was 83 % of pre-war. West Germany had set a goal of 107 % of pre-war level in agriculture and this necessitated considerable increase in fertilizer and the use of new methods.

Financial stability was good. Wholesale prices reflected the increase of import costs but the readjustment after the currency devaluation was largely restricted to the higher cost of imports from dollar areas. Employment was at a high level, except for the expellees in West Germany. Some progress had been made in absorbing them into the life of West

Germany, but Berlin still reported 25 % of its labor force unemployed but this was the result of continuing immigration. Technical assistance continued to increase. A total of $ 7,341,000 was approved for this item for the quarter, with Greece receiving $ 4,457,300, United Kingdom $ 999,400, Turkey $ 800,700 and other smaller amounts. The end of civil war in Greece and its urgent needs for recovery were the reason for its large allotment. By the end of March, 1950, ECA had allotted $ 8,984,900,000 since April 1948; procurements authorized from January to March 1950 amounted to $ 704,100,000 with United Kingdom receiving $ 165,000,000, France $ 141,400,000, Netherlands $ 95,300,000, Italy $ 91,000,000 and Germany only $ 38,500,000. But Germany was the beneficiary of the GARIOA funds in this quarter and they amounted to $ 187,000,000. The total ECA counterpart funds deposited now totaled the equivalent of $ 5,660,000,000 since April 1948; ECA had approved the withdrawal of $ 335,000,000 for use by the participating countries in this quarter. Threefourths of this was used for capital investment, relief and housing. No funds were used for monetary stabilization. The largest amounts in Germany went to building power plants, rebuilding railways and industrial plants and assisting agriculture. ECA had approved 161,000,000 DM credits for business firms ($ 38,000,000). Since the beginning of 1949 ECA had approved more than 1,400,000,000 DM, allotted to investment projects, and about 1/3 to pay German exporters for goods shipped to ERP countries under drawing rights [5]).

The Fourth Quarter — 1 April to 30 June 1950
Need for Military Expansion

The sudden break of the Korean War required military expansion which would have been impossible if the European economic base had not been expanded. The industrial production in the second quarter of 1950 was at the peak with 124 % of the pre-war level. The volume of intra-European trade had increased from 90 % of pre-war levels in 1949 to 115 % in the first half of 1950. The European Payments Union had contributed to ERP and to the development of a single competitive market in Western Europe and to the convertibility of currencies, thus preparing the way for economic integration and the reduction of discriminating trade barriers.

The increased industrial production in most of the participating countries brought problems of manpower. The leading industrial nations were short of labor and many of the others had widespread unemployment. The OEEC came to an agreement that there should be a redistribution of labor and six nations — Belgium, France, Italy, Luxembourg, Netherlands and United Kingdom agreed to: 1) Facilitate movement of workers for temporary residence; 2) Provide assistance to indigent workers; 3) Provide arrangements so that workers moving from one country to another could carry accumulated rights to social benefits. Italy and Belgium had negotiated to insure such rights. The International Labor Organization held a conference in April 1950 to discuss the problems involved. On June 27, 1950 the President of the United States authorized the ECA to contribute $ 1,000,000 toward the technical assistance of such labor migrations. The OEEC sponsored a project in this area and the participating nations paid for it. The I.L.O. administered it. The purpose was: 1) to train staffs; 2) to develop techniques, and 3) establish demonstration projects for operating model employment offices, reception centers, and training methods. Upon this effort and the experience derived Germany was later able to recruit workers for its rapidly expanding industrial progress.

By 1950 a growing public interest in ERP was evident, along with increasing sense of community and a recognition of the necessity of more unification, and finally a focusing of sentiment on the central political issue, namely, Communist imperialism. Since April, 1948 $ 9,500,000,000 of purchases had been authorized by ECA with GARIOA increasing it to $ 9,800,000,000. The index of industrial production continued to rise for all countries and it had gone from 97 in 1948, 115 in 1949, to 124 in the 2nd quarter of 1950. For Germany, it had gone from 41 in 1948 to 74 in 1949 and 90 in 1950 [6]).

The chief feature in industrial development was the rapid increase in automobile manufacture. The production for this quarter was 100 % above the first quarter of 1950, and 40 % above the same period in 1949. The increased volume was chiefly the result of production in Germany, France and Italy.

There was the promise of another good harvest in 1950. Meat was still below pre-war levels, but dairy products were up to the 1938 level. In general, prices were stable and currencies strengthened in relation to the dollar; reserves of gold and dollars had increased.

Exports — Imports

Exports from Western Europe rose to a new high of 121 % of the pre-war levels. Compared to earlier European trade deficits, the United States now showed a decline of $ 145,500,000 per month in 1950. The production of steel had increased slightly, but there had been a readjustment in that industry. In West Germany, where the level of industry agreement had limited the production of steel previous to the establishment of the Federal Republic, now steel production suddenly increased by 23 % over the previous year. These increases were offset by declines in Luxembourg, France including the Saar, and Belgium. Coal production was seasonally lower, approximately 108,000,000 tons against 114,000,000, but compared with the same period of the previous year, it showed a gain of 2,000,000 metric tons. The Coal Committee of the OEEC recognized the improvement in the coal situation by suspending allocations for the third quarter of 1950.

United States world trade had decreased further, and European countries had accumulated a $ 1,300,000,000 trade balance in nine months. The participating countries improved their foreign exchange positions by: 1) reducing hard currency liabilities; 2) by cutting debt on payments accounts, and 3) by improving their soft currency positions. Intra-European trade rose from 19 % of pre-war levels during the first half of 1949 to 115 % in the first half of 1950. A considerable part of the increase among OEEC nations was attributable to the resumption by Germany of her traditional position of supplier of manufactured goods to Western Europe. Efforts by ECA to encourage exports of ERP countries to the United States followed two lines: 1) the ultimate development of a high steady consumption of European products, and 2) the removal of artificial barriers to the importation of such goods. During this quarter ECA assisted the effort by 1) determining articles with the greatest sales appeal in the United States and estimating quantities which might be sold; 2) analyzing problems encountered in selling the United States market; 3) assisting in the preparations to stage trade-fair exhibits of foreign goods; 4) bringing to the attention of the Committee for Reprocity Information requests for concessions; 5) resolving with the Bureau of Customs problems of classification and procedures which were alleged to be impeding imports; 6) survey of problems of financing exports to the United States; 7) arranging technical assistance market surveys; 8) bringing to the attention of foreign nationals the advantages of using the facilities of the six foreign trade zones in the United States.

Liberalizing Trade

The effect of devaluation and liberalization of currencies was that prices rose moderately and European currencies were brought into better balance among the participating countries, restoring more realistic price levels. The efforts to liberalize trade by removing arbitrary restrictions on imports brought an increase in European trade. Germany liberalized its imports more than any other one of the countries. Consequently, Germany which had been a creditor, became a very heavy debtor in the European Payments Union. OEEC made repeated shifts in the trade and payments position. Germany, which had no drawing rights under the 1949—50 agreement, was assigned $ 12,000,000 in May 1950 and carried over $ 60,300,000 in bilateral drawing rights from the agreement of 1948—49. The new European Payments Union Agreement was significant for the future trade in Europe since it capitalized on the experience of the earlier Plan. It was designed to promote the free flow of intra-European trade through a fully automatic multilateral system which permits each member to offset its deficit with any other country. Debtor countries were required to reduce the country's deficit by making dollar or gold payments. The OEEC countries committed themselves to further reduction of quantitative restriction on intra-European trade. All discriminating restrictions were to end 1 January 1951. The new European Payments Union was due to start 20 September 1950. The United States provided $ 350,000,000 to provide working capital and a special assistance fund to aid countries which encountered serious difficulties. The sterling area credits were transferable. The United Kingdom was insured against heavy dollar drain. The European Payments Union was handled by a Management Committee of seven members set up under the authority of OEEC. Rates of exchange were administered by the central banks;

set up under authority of OEEC; each bank was to report to the Bank of International Settlement, the agent of E.P.U.

The liberalization of intra-European trade was begun with a 50 % target set for 15 December 1949. 60 % on food and raw materials and manufactured goods was set by 31 January 1950 and 75 % by 31 January 1951. Members were expected to complain to OEEC if there was discrimination. A European Integration Fund was established to receive net contributions from countries which gain initially to reimburse those who incur losses in the change.

Schuman Plan Proposed

The Schuman Plan was proposed 9 May 1950 to pool coal and steel industries of France and Germany, with an invitation to other countries to join. The purpose was 1) to advance political rapproachment of Germany with the rest of Europe through a supra-national high authority to which member countries would delegate their control over coal and steel industries; and 2) to create a more nearly competitive market for the two industries. This high authority might forestall international steel cartels that prevented the best use of Europe's steel capacity during the inter-war period. One of the outstanding political questions was the degree to which national governments would be permitted to influence the decisions of the authority. Britain did not share in the discussion but expressed an interest in the plan. The principle of European economic integration was warmly supported by the ECA because of its importance to the prosperity and survival of Western Europe. This was the beginning of a series of unification efforts.

ECA Procurements

The ECA approved procurement authorizations of $ 775,000,000 in this quarter bringing the total since April 1948 to $ 10,232,500,000 available and $ 9,793,000,000 allotted. Of this quarter allotment, Germany received $ 55,100,000; $ 2,200,000 in food, feed and fertilizer, $ 4,800,000 in fuel, $ 33,400,000 in raw materials and semi-finished products, $ 5,200,000 in machinery and vehicles, $ 13,200,000 in miscellaneous items including tobacco, ocean freight and technical services.

The industrial production indexes for all Europe [7]), including West Germany, continued at 124, without Germany, it was 137. Germany's index had risen from 83 to 90. In the second quarter of 1950 participating nations deposited the equivalent of $ 766,000,000 in local currencies in the counterpart funds, and received approval to withdraw the equivalent of $ 414,000,000 for special projects in their own countries. Counterpart fund approvals since April 1948 had amounted to the equivalent of $ 4,333,000,000; promotion of production $ 2,573,000,000; $ 1,114,000,000 debt retirement and $ 646,000,000 for other projects. Almost one-third of the funds used for promotion of production was spent on building new power plants. In this period, Germany received $ 464,000,000 DM for the investment program channeled into agriculture, housing construction, electric power plants, industrial production, transportation and communication equipment, tourism, and care for refugees and aid to Berlin.

[1]) This material is quoted from the Fourth ECA Report, p. 22—25, see the Report to Congress, Economic Cooperation Administration, 1 January to 31 March 1949.

[2]) p. 34, Seventh Report to Congress, Economic Cooperation Administration, 1 October to 31 December 1949.

[3]) cf. p. 8—9, Eighth Report to Congress, 1 January to 31 March 1950, Economic Cooperation Administration, U. S. Government Printing Office.

[4]) cf. p. 22, Eighth Report to Congress, 1 January to 31 March 1950, Economic Cooperation Administration, U. S. Government Printing Office.

[5]) cf. p. 56—57, Eighth Report to Congress, Economic Cooperation Administration, U. S. Government Printing Office.

[6]) cf. p. 6, Ninth Report to Congress, Economic Cooperation Administration, U. S. Government Printing Office.

[7]) cf. p. 109, Industrial Production Indexes from Ninth Report to Congress, Economic Cooperation Administration, April — June 1950, U. S. Government Printing Office.

Chapter V

THE THIRD YEAR OF THE MARSHALL PLAN

Progress of ERP

The remarkable progress of the European Recovery Program during the first two and one-half years made it possible to undertake the rearmament necessary for Europe to resist the threat to survival of free nations. Military developments really increased the need for a unified European market. There was some concern that the accelerated defense production and increase in military forces might be carried out at the expense of living standards of lower income groups in the European nations. The Korean War had involved many nations around the world; this and other threats brought about the organization of the North Atlantic Treaty Organization and its armed forces. The immediate effect of the Korean War was: 1) to remove all doubt that the United States would defend the peace against military aggression; 2) to prove that the United States would work through the United Nations; 3) to bring home to Europeans the magnitude of the Soviet purposes and the inadequacies of their own defenses; and 4) to have the assurance that armament needs would not be allowed to sacrifice economic gains. These facts brought a new solidarity to the participating nations in the OEEC.

The First Quarter — 1 July to 30 September 1950

The Western Europe combined index of industrial production advanced another 13 % in this current quarter over the same quarter in 1949. The September index [1]) was 133 % of the pre-war level. The international financial position of the European nations was greatly improved; government revenues and exports soared. The Korean War put such burdens upon the United States that export dollar aid dropped to $ 295,000,000 for the quarter. The fear of inflation developed a scramble for goods and stocks. There was need for OEEC to plan for unified operations and the maintenance of stability.

Industrial Production Indexes, 1946—50
(1938 — 100)

Country	1946	1947	1948	1949	1950
Total	77	87	101	115	127
Excluding Western Germany	94	107	120	129	139
Austria	46	55	85	113	134
Belgium	91	106	114	116	120
Denmark	103	119	133	142	157
France	79	95	111	122	123
Germany (Fed. Rep.)	29	34	51	75	95
Greece	55	69	76	90	113
Ireland	112	120	132	144	160
Italy	75	95	99	105	119
Luxembourg	86	109	145	139	146
Netherlands	74	94	113	126	139
Norway	100	115	124	132	142
Sweden	139	142	151	158	166
Turkey	135	153	154	161	—
United Kingdom	106	114	128	137	149

Although the Table A-1 shows the quarter average at 97 for Germany, in fact, it rose to 105 in September of this period, exceeding the pre-war level for the first time. Steel production rose to 12,300,000 metric tons. Germany was chiefly responsible for the European 10 % increase by its advance of 34 % in its own steel production. Motor vehicle production was at a new high; coal shortages appeared again and shipments from the United States were necessary to keep up with the new industrial pace. Unemployment was 35 % below the previous low in February 1950.

Agriculture was 109 compared with the 1938 level of 100. Food imports had dropped but Western Europe still needed to import about one-third of its food supplies. The ECA exchange of workers introduced European farmers to American agricultural methods. In May 1950, the Grassland Conference was held by the OEEC in an attempt to increase pasturage for beef production.

Financial stability seemed to be established. Gold and dollar reserves increased $ 700,000,000 during the third quarter in addition to the $ 1,000,000,000 in the first half of 1950. Wholesale prices had increased approximately 8 % in Europe, the same as in the United States. The

United States world trade changed considerably with exports dropping and imports increasing, thus altering the unfavorable European trade balance which had impeded progress for years since the war. From the first quarter of 1949, when the United States had a trade balance of $ 1,535,000,000, it declined to $ 60,000,000 in the third quarter of 1950. Of course, the Korean War had much to do with this.

Economic Unification

In Europe there had been much progress toward economic unification. Trade liberalization measures were important and urgent. Intra-European trade continued to grow, and there was some danger of unwarranted export controls. OEEC's program for liberalization of trade had proceeded with the 50 % free list achieved on 2 November 1949, the 60 % goal on 4 October 1950, with plans for the 75 % list to be achieved on 1 February 1951. The success of these liberalization measures depended on the competence and vigor of the Special Committee in charge and acceptance by the participating countries.

The Schuman Plan for the consolidation of the coal and steel industries was being developed with the details of this economic integration. The European Payments Union agreement had been signed on 19 September 1950 retroactive to July. It provided for special problems of multilateral trade clearances such as: 1) the unexpectedly large deficit of Germany that would have required the paying of nearly $ 31,000,000 in gold to EPU; 2) an unusually large deficit of the Netherlands which completely exhausted the initial credit allotted by EPU; and the heavy surplus of France requiring gold payment by EPU of nearly $ 41,000,000. The German deficit resulted from the excess of import purchases immediately after the release of Germany from Military Government regulations and the freedom under the new Federal Republic to spend money again. These problems were worked out satisfactorily without serious inconvenience to the countries involved, or others.

The ECA allotted the participating countries a total of $ 2,700,000,000 for the current quarter along with an additional $ 500,000,000. Most of the procurements were for raw materials and semi-finished products comprising 44 %, and food, feed and fertilizer for 24 %. GARIOA funds were turned over to ECA at this time so that there was $ 187,000,000 to be used for procurements and shipping costs. Authorizations against the GARIOA were $ 181,200,000 which completed the special program for Germany started by the United States Army. Among the special projects for Germany this quarter was an oil refinery at Lingen with an output projected at 600,000 metric tons per year of gasoline, diesel oil and coke. Technical assistance at the end of 30 September 1950 amounted to $ 17,400,000 chiefly in the industrial (42 %) and agricultural (15 %) areas. Investment guarantees continued with 23 new contracts amounting to $ 23,000,000.

Counterpart Funds

During this quarter the equivalent of $ 733,000,000 was deposited by the participating countries in local currency counterpart funds to match aid by the United States. The total since 1948 amounted to the equivalent of $ 7,200,000,000 with approved withdrawal of $ 544,000,000 during this quarter. The use of the counterpart funds stressed strategic materials and this resulted in a number of exploration contracts in colonial possessions in Asia and Africa. Almost ³/₅ of the strategic materials contracts were with the United Kingdom for its commonwealth countries, and France and the Netherlands accounted for most of the remainder. In this quarter, Germany received the largest allotment — the equivalent of $ 84,400,000 was earmarked for financing manufacture, farming, power facilities and other projects to stimulate production. The rest was allotted to financing housing construction for workers, to promote tourism and to pay for inland transportation of relief package shipments with building of new power plants. West Berlin had become practically independent of the Soviet Zone for electricity. Of the 5 % of the counterpart funds which was reserved for the United States amounting to the equivalent of $ 309,000,000 by 30 September 1950, $ 121,000,000 had been expended by the ECA for its own expense and for use by the U.S. Government agencies for stock-piling strategic materials. For the new Mutual Defense Assistance Program Congress appropriated $ 4,000,000,000 for the year 1951. $ 475,000,000 for the current quarter was to be used by Western European countries to expand defense production in collaboration with the ECA.

The Second Quarter — 1 October to 31 December 1950
The Economic Base of Defense

The economic foundation, i.e. economic stability so necessary to national defense, became apparent in this last quarter of 1950. Production went up 10 %; exports rose sharply; unemployment was stable; retail prices held steady in spite of demand; West Europe's trade balance improved markedly and holdings of dollars and gold rose. Nevertheless, production had to increase even more if programs for defense were to be met without reducing living standards. The NATO group found that there had already been a 20 % rise in defense costs. Measures against inflation had to be devised and met with public investment programs if necessary and even controls over imports and exports. To guide this, NATO nations — Belgium, Denmark, France, Iceland, Italy, Luxembourg, Netherlands, Norway, Portugal and the United Kingdom, — set up the NATO Defense Production Board.

Industrial production for all of Europe in this period moved up from 122 in the previous quarter to 139 in this one [2]). This meant a substantial increase over the pre-war level. West Germany's index, although low in certain areas, had climbed to 110 % — a 37 % increase from the same quarter in 1949. The largest gain by West Germany was in steel; Italy and Austria also made large gains. Britain gained only 5 %. The greater industrial activity required more imports of coal from the United States.

Agriculture increased 30 % over the 1947—48 level. It was apparent that investment in Europe was not likely to develop agriculture to the point where imports would not be necessary. There had been a noticeable increase in the use of fertilizers, greater use of grassland, and efforts to combat disease in livestock, as well as improved grades of seed. Yet, these were not enough.

Increased Stability

Financial stability had increased remarkably. Earnings from "invisibles" flowed to the participating countries. Gold and dollar reserves increased $ 500,000,000 in the October—December quarter. Since devaluation in September 1949 reserves had grown to $ 2,400,000,000; the largest gain was in the United Kingdom, $ 1,900,000,000. Wholesale prices had been increasing. Retail prices rose slowly. There was some imposition of controls and agreements for allocation of scarce materials with the hope of steadying prices. By the end of 1950 workers in most European countries had regained or passed their pre-war wage levels, but they were still low. It was true that pressure for wage increases had grown. Then too, 11 % of the workers in West Germany were still unemployed and the OEEC undertook further efforts to redeploy labor.

Foreign trade exports in Western Europe stood at 157 % of the 1938 level and the average monthly rate passed the previous second quarter index. Imports did not rise so fast, but prices of raw materials were rising. This emphasized the value of the EPU. This fourth quarter trade was 16 % higher than the preceding quarter and 34 % higher than the same quarter in 1949. The total value of exports from the participating countries averaged $ 2,000,000,000 per month at post-devaluation rates. The greatest increases were in West Germany, France, Belgium, Netherlands, and the United Kingdom. In this quarter, participating countries imported at the rate of $ 2,300,000,000 per month. Imports from non-participating countries declined from $ 1,200,000,000 to $ 1,000,000,000 per month, whereas exports from participating countries rose from $ 900,000,000 to $ 1,300,000,000 per month. Imports from the United States and Canada dropped to $ 300,000,000 per month in the last quarter of 1950. The trade deficit with the Western Hemisphere dropped from $ 290,000,000 to $ 160,000,000 [3]). Germany's exports in this quarter rose 38 % over the same quarter in 1949.

The EPU operation showed disproportions due to radical change on world trade patterns. The main problems were France's surplus in sterling and Germany's continuing trade deficit. Germany accounted for one-half the total imbalance at the end of December 1950. By that time, West Germany had exhausted its EPU quota principally because of large payments in sterling. The Board of EPU undertook a special study and Germany submitted a plan to cancel the outstanding import licenses and offered a 50 % deposit against the value of these licenses, also higher taxes and tighter credit. The result was that West Germany received an extra EPU credit of $ 120,000,000 units of account. This was to cover 2/3 of the German deficit and 1/3 to be paid to EPU by 1 July 1951 in liquidation of the owners' deficit. It is interesting to note that by 31 December 1950 EPU had drawn only $ 42,700,000 of the $ 350,000,000 advanced by the United States when the Union started.

Trade Liberalization

The trade liberalization measures undertaken by the OEEC brought the participating countries closer together; the defense needs promoted this unity even further.

Trade Liberalization, intra-European Imports [4])
(31 December 1950 — % of 1948 Imports)

Country	Total	Raw Material	Food & Feed	Mfg. Goods
United Kingdom	86	91	80	84
Italy	76	82	73	66
Sweden	69	77	61	65
Greece	67	71	67	62
Austria	66	87	44	52
France	66	73	61	60
Belgium-Luxembourg	65	74	60	60
Germany	65	70	65	60
Ireland	65	82	60	61
Netherlands	63	67	62	60
Switzerland	62	63	60	63
Portugal	61	60	69	61
Turkey	60	64	75	59
Denmark	50	81	59	25
Norway	45	84	68	29
Iceland	14	—	—	—

The OEEC at this time was pushing the 60 % level with the hope that all countries might reach this degree of free trade at an early date. The target date for the 75 % level was set at 28 February 1951. It was generally recognized that a greater degree of economic efficiency could be achieved by removal of discrimination in trade. The Schuman Plan had progressed to the point that France, Belgium, Luxembourg, Netherlands, West Germany and Italy had agreed to merge their domestic markets for coal and steel into a single unit with an authority in control. The date set for the final ratification of the treaty was 19 March 1951. This meant the elimination of cartels and the encouragement of free competition in these countries.

63

Since 9 April 1948 ECA had made $ 12,300,000,000 available for European recovery with $ 463,000,000 obligated for the October—December 1950 quarter. The previous quarter was $ 500,000,000 of which $ 350,000,000 was allotted as working capital. This applied to all countries participating except the United Kingdom where condition had improved so greatly that all allotments were cancelled. Britain planned to remain a member of OEEC however. The countries of origin for supplies were the United States — 69 % of all commodities; 12 % from Canada and 8 % from Latin America, and the remaining 3 % from various countries.

Counterpart Funds

Local currency counterpart funds continued to grow. The various participating nations had deposited $ 516,000,000 during the last quarter of 1950; this was about 1/3 less than the previous quarter. Since April 1948, $ 7,600,000,000 had been paid in. There had been $ 7,300,000,000 released for use including the GARIOA funds. Most of this was for rehabilitation, industrial improvement, transportation, mining, electric power and expansion of manufacture. Some went to health and housing. Germany's share also included the funds made available for Berlin aid. The United States share 5 % of the counterpart funds was $ 333,000,000, about half used by ECA for administration and $ 89,000,000 for the purchase of raw materials for U.S. stock-pile. Of these, approximately 60 % was by purchase with counterpart funds and the remainder direct cash purchases.

The Third Quarter — 1 January to 31 March 1951
Rise of Defense Spending

With the coming of the first calendar quarter of 1951, the ECA program for West Europe was further adapted to securing for that area the economic strength needed to advance its mobilization plan and to hold its hard-won living standard. NATO was being built up; in two years of military build-up, the rate of military production had more than doubled. Expenses for national defense had risen sharply because of the shortage of raw materials. It was averaging 38 % above the pre-war level and a gain of 13 % from 1950. Of course, taxes and government expense had risen, too.

Important economic gains had to be held if military needs were to be met. With respect to national capacity for defense in relation to gross national product, Europe's was about $ 566 per person compared with $ 1,985 for the United States. The cost of defense per capita in Europe was $ 530 while that of the United States was $ 1,840 per capita. Since late 1950, ECA had become a claimant agency with expanded activities to provide for essential import requirements of the participating countries and their over-seas territories. It had compiled detailed statements of commodity requirements for each country. ECA had financed a program of rationing to be administered by various agencies and it was operating in steel, non-ferrous metals, sulphur, cotton and chemicals. Europe still had to depend on the United States for essential items, and needed ECA to help provide them.

The industrial production index in Western Europe had risen to average 39 % above the pre-war levels and 13 % above the first quarter of 1950. The largest gain was in Germany, namely 34 %, and Greece was second with 27 %. All countries had increased over 1950. OEEC had been attempting to increase the efficiency of steel production. Coal production was up 500,000 metric tons per month more than the last quarter in 1950 and 700,000 metric tons above the first quarter of 1950, but the demands for coal had grown to the point where it was again necessary to ship coal from the United States. The electric power output was below needs in spite of its recent expansion and counterpart funds were being approved to provide further expansion. Motor vehicle output in Germany, France and Italy was up 50—60 %. In agriculture, the slow growth was still short of needs and imports were required to provide for necessary supplies. Manpower problems varied; Germany still had considerable unemployment but other countries were short-handed. OEEC was making plans to recruit labor from areas where there was unemployment.

Foreign Trade

Foreign trade had increased steadily. Participating countries in 1951 had increased their exports from $ 4,984,000,000 in the first quarter of 1949 to $ 6,063,000,000 in the first quarter 1951, while their imports had increased from $ 6,314,000,000 to $ 7,734,000,000 in the same period. Their trade with the rest of the world showed exports at $ 2,746,000,000 for 1949 and $ 3,013,000,000 in 1951 with imports at $ 4,155,000,000 in 1949 and $ 4,651,000,000 in 1951 [5]). The balance of payments was still strong against Europe and the help of ECA was needed. Intra-European trade was 22 % higher than a year earlier. A great need for raw materials had developed. To meet this need there was a sharp increase in imports from the United States, — $ 3,000,000,000 for the first quarter 1951 against $ 2,600,000,000 in the 4th quarter of 1950. Much of this advance was due to higher prices. Exports had also increased in European trade with America, in amount $ 3,300,000,000, the highest since 1949. As to financial stability, the wholesale prices were up 10—20 %; retail prices were up 20 %. There was a considerable increase in dollar and gold holdings. EPU's multilateral clearings had raised the volume of intra-European trade. West Germany still posed a problem deficit and that government had to cut liberalization to reduce imports and also the volume of lending to regulate and allocate all raw materials. It is interesting to note that the German position reversed itself in March and registered a surplus. Austria, Denmark and Turkey experienced deficits in March and had to settle partially in gold. EPU had continued to receive more gold or dollars than it had to pay out and had continued to avoid using the American credit.

Coal & Steel Authority

The Schuman Plan for the control of steel and coal was completed by the signing of the agreement on 18 April 1951 with Belgium, Luxembourg, France, West Germany, Italy and the Netherlands transferring their national control to the new Coal and Steel Authority. The essential provisions of the plan were: 1) An Executive Body — the High Authority of 9 members chosen by the Council of Ministers strictly on the basis of their qualifications; 2) The Council of Ministers — to initiate and review decisions specified by the High Authority; 3) The Common Assembly — appointed by Parliaments of the member nations to approve the budget and review activities; 4) The Court of Justice — to hear appeals from enterprise or government of alleged violations of the treaty; and 5) A Consultative Committee to provide contact between the High Authority and the producer, the laborer, and the consumer. The economic provisions were: 1) All tariffs, import restrictions, subsidies, discrimination in freight rates and double pricing practiced on coal and steel must be removed between the participating countries; 2) Agreements and mergers between firms and joint selling agencies designed to reduce competition are prohibited; 3) The High Authority may veto investments that would require discriminatory subsidies; 4) The High Authority may allocate coal and steel products and supplies and control prices on short range; price floors may be imposed in times of crisis; 5) The High Authority will conduct negotiations on revisions for tariffs on coal and steel imports; 6) The High Authority will supervise fair wages and employment practices in both industries, also move workers across boundaries when necessary; 7) Certain exceptions remained to enable the High Authority to stabilize operations. The Plan was one of the high points in the development of cooperation in the economic field of Western Europe.

The ECA allotted $ 445,000,000 to participating countries for this quarter making a total of $ 12,300,000,000 appropriated since 1948. Like Britain, Ireland withdrew its request for aid because its progress made it unnecessary but remained a member of OEEC and the EPU. The main source of supplies was still the United States with 70 %. The Technical Assistance Program had been growing steadily and Europe was profiting greatly from this aid. Dollar equivalent local currencies (counterpart funds) payments of $ 6,400,000,000 had been used as approved and planned. The 5 % reserved for the United States amounted to $ 359,000,000; $ 157,000,000 had been used by the ECA for administration and $ 50,000,000 transferred to the U.S. Treasury for payment to various government agencies and an uncommitted balance of $ 152,000,000 remained, probably for purchase of raw materials of strategic use.

The Fourth Quarter — 1 April to 30 June 1951
Continuing Growth

There was continuing need of aid to advance the Military Defense Assistance Program. Shortages of basic materials were serious. Furthermore, every available step had to be taken to maintain financial stability and to aggregate supply and demand. The OEEC planned an aggressive offensive against the inflation and self-help measures were initiated. Western Europe's expanding economic base still increased. The gain in industrial production was 14 % over 1950 6). The largest gains were in Austria, Belgium, Germany, Italy and Greece, ranging from 16 to 29 % up. German production rose to a new high in this quarter, 21 % over 1950. Coal production in Germany showed the largest gain, 13 % above 1950. Agriculture increased little. Consumption was 40 % above the pre-war level because of an increased population. Employment was expanding in all countries. The larger need for raw materials raised the value of imports from the rest of the world to $ 1,800,000,000 in the quarter, — a record high. This was 18 % increase over the previous quarter and 51 % over the same time in 1950. The volume also increased 90 % over the previous quarter, 15 % over 1950. The intra-European trade was up as was that with the United States. As far as price stability was concerned, there was a sudden down-turn in the prices of basic raw materials and this caused a halt to wholesale price increases. The EPU noted reverse trends, with United Kingdom, France and Portugal running deficits and West Germany showing a stable surplus which paid off all special credits advanced by EPU in the past. Eight countries had met the 75 % standard for liberalization of imports. Germany met the 60 % stage but was not required to meet the 75 % level at this time. Since the earlier time, when Germany tried to meet this standard, and had to abandon it, conditions had improved and a new import program was being developed to meet this new level soon.

This was the third year of the Marshall Plan. Progress had been noteworthy, and participating countries of OEEC were well on their way to economic independence. Moreover, the experience of working together toward an integrated European economic system was inspiring. European leaders were glimpsing the possible benefits of effective unity in building a permanent union of people who had been enemies for centuries.

[1] cf. p. 103 (Adapted from Table A-1) Industrial Production Index, 1946—50, Tenth Annual Report to Congress, Economic Cooperation Administration, U. S. Government Printing Office.

[2] cf. p. 103, Table A-1, Eleventh Report to Congress, Economic Cooperation Administration, U. S. Government Printing Office.

[3] cf. Table A-8 Appendix Eleventh Report to Congress, Economic Cooperation Administration, 1 October to 31 December 1950, U. S. Government Printing Office.

[4] cf. p. 32 — Trade liberalization, intra-European imports, 31 December 1950, Economic Cooperation Administration.

[5] cf. p. 22, Twelfth Report to Congress, 1 January to 31 March 1951, Economic Cooperation Administration.

[6] cf. p. 17, Thirteenth Report to Congress, 1 April to 30 June 1951, Economic Cooperation Administration.

Chapter VI

THE FOURTH YEAR OF THE MARSHALL PLAN

The Mutual Security Agency
1951—1952

The Effect of War in Korea

While the original plan for the European Recovery Program was scheduled on a four year period, changing conditions in the world made adjustments necessary. Chief among these was the Korean War which the United Nations had been forced to fight because of the invasion by the North Korean Army into South Korea. Although the United States carried most of the military and financial burden of this conflict, all nations inevitably became involved to a greater or less extent. The North Atlantic Treaty Organization had revitalized the military potential of Western Europe and this had involved a massive increase in military equipment. Fortunately the European Recovery Program had gone well and the Western European nations were able to undertake this added economic burden without serious difficulty. Nevertheless, all the participating nations in the ERP had to alter their original plans and stress the new need for military manpower and weapons. Consequently, the ECA had begun to change its primary mission in the year 1950—1951 and after the American Congress had passed a bill merging the economic activities of the Economic Cooperation Administration and Mutual Security Agency, the emphasis 'became more and more a military one. Hence, the fourth year of the Marshall Plan was completely altered to divert the resources of European nations to the needs and demands of NATO as an active defense operation. This chapter will, therefore, indicate the changed nature of the ECA and actually the phasing out of the original plans.

Combined ECA — MSA

Many features of the ECA were retained by the MSA, particularly as they pertained to the economic factors necessary for the support of a new military task. At the end of 3¹/₂ years of the Marshall Plan the United States had laid out $ 12,000,000,000 instead of the $ 17,000,000,000 which had been projected for the four year program. In this period, Western Europe had increased its industrial output to 35 % above the pre-war level of 1938, and exports to the rest of the world 50 % above that level. The First Report to Congress by the Mutual Security Agency, 31 December 1951, stated: "The structural underpinnings of European recovery had been restored. The Marshall Plan was not just an economic success, it helped to create political stability as well" [1]). The basic components of Military Security were outlined as: 1) Direct contributions to military equipment; 2) Raw materials, commodities and machinery to support military effort; 3) Economic and technical contribution necessary to support military build-up.

The Mutual Security Agency (MSA) actually completed the aid measures initiated under the ECA in essentially the same manner previously used. The MSA Act of 1951 provided aid not only to the NATO countries but to all those which had participated in the European Recovery Program. The organization administering this changed program was essentially the same as that set up by the ECA. The OEEC in Paris remained the same representative unit of the participating nations. The joint headquarters of MSA and ECA in Washington cleared aid in much the same manner as before. The administrative machinery for West Germany, for instance, was typical of the other nations. The Federal Ministry for the Marshall Plan, in Bonn, handled affairs; it had the Mission of the Federal Republic of Germany to the OEEC in Paris; it also had a Mission in Washington to ECA/MSA; the ECA/MSA maintained its Special Mission in Bonn; there was also the Office of the Special Representative in Paris with contacts at Washington and Paris [2]).

Allotments for 1951—1952

The Report for the last year of ECA, 1951—1952, is necessarily abbreviated by the fact that it was combined with the MSA, just beginning. The allotments to participant countries for the 1951—1952 year for ECA and MSA were $ 1,486,200,000, of which Britain received $ 350,000,000, France $ 261,500,000, Greece $ 178,800,000, Italy $ 159,300,000, Austria $ 116,000,000, Netherlands $ 100,000,000, Germany $ 91,700,000, and the remainder to other countries. European counterpart funds continued to be handled as they were under ECA. The deposits in these local currency accounts amounted to $ 1,570,800,000 in dollar equivalents, which added to what was carried over, totaled $ 2,966,000,000 available for approval. The total approved for withdrawal was $ 1,665,000,000. Of this, Germany had a balance from previous years of $ 88,000,000, deposits in the current of $ 148,500,000, making a total available for approval of $ 236,500,000, of which $ 166,400,000 was approved [3]).

Foreign trade had remained fairly stable in this year 1951—1952. Reports show that the intra-European trade index was 189 in 1950—51 and 182 in 1951—52; the imports to OEEC countries from the rest of the world were 103 in 1950—51, as contrasted with 113 in 1951—52; exports to the rest of the world rated at 160 in 1950—51 and 168 in 1951—52 [4]). (1948 was used as base of 100 and these figures indicate comparison in volume.) The combined index of the OEEC countries in export trade of OEEC with non-OEEC areas was 570 for the second quarter of 1950; 892 for the second quarter of 1951 and 843 for the same quarter in 1952. (These figures are the monthly average in millions of dollars equivalent.) The imports showed similar trends. The combined index of the OEEC countries was 945 for 1950, second quarter; 1433 for the second quarter 1951; and 1253 for the second quarter 1952 [5]). Europe still showed an unfavorable trade balance considering the amount of material imported from the United States. All of these reveal a healthy and favorable advance in the OEEC countries during the four years of the ECA plan.

Review of Four Years of the Marshall Plan

Since 1951—1952 was the last year of the Marshall Plan, it may be desirable to introduce a summary of the progress that developed in the participating countries of the OEEC during the four years. This will be done largely by tables with the totals for all and special figures for some of the larger European countries in detail, omitting the others.

ECA/MSA — Allotments to all Member Countries between 3 April 1948 — 31 December 1952

(million $)

Country	cumulative through Dec. 31, 1952	broken down by fiscal years				
		1948/49 (15 months)	1949/50	1950/51	1951/52	1952/53 (through Dec. 31, 1952)
Total	13,908.9	5,953.0	3,523.0	2,405.9	1,486.2	540.8
of which:						
Great Britain	3,442.8	1,619.7	907.9	298.4	350.0	266.9
France	2,806.3	1,313.4	698.3	433.1	261.5	100.0
Italy	1,515.0	668.0	403.7	244.0	159.3	40.0
Germany, Federal Republic	1,412.8	613.5	284.7	399.1	91.7	23.8
Netherlands excl. Indonesia	977.3	507.0	268.3	101.9	100.0	—
Austria	711.8	280.0	166.5	114.3	116.0	35.0
Greece	693.9	191.7	156.3	167.1	178.8	—
Belgium-Luxembourg	555.5	261.4	210.9	74.3	8.9	—
Denmark	275.9	126.2	86.1	45.1	14.0	4.5
Norway	253.5	101.1	89.5	46.1	16.8	—
Turkey	242.5	49.0	58.5	45.0	70.0	20.0
Yugoslavia	159.3	—	—	29.0	80.3	50.0
Ireland	146.2	86.3	44.9	15.0	—	—
Sweden	107.1	45.4	51.9	21.2	11.4	—
Indonesia	101.4	64.1	37.3	—	—	—
Portugal	50.5	—	38.8	11.7	—	—
Trieste	32.6	17.9	12.5	2.1	—	—
Iceland	29.8	8.3	7.0	8.4	5.5	0.6
General freight account	33.5	—	—	—	33.5	—
EPU-capital fund	361.4	—	—	350.0	11.4	—

(Adapted from page 4, Mutual Security Program, Report to Congress, December 1952)

Germany received about 10 % of the total aid granted, although this country was under the restrictions of Military Government from April 3, 1948 when the European Recovery Program started, until October 1949, when the three West Zones were united and established as the Federal Republic of Germany. At that time, West Germany became a member of the Organization for European Economic Cooperation and shared fully in the planning and operation of the Program.

Like all European countries, a large part of the assistance in the early years was devoted to food and agricultural products and fuel because these were urgently needed items at that time. Furthermore, since Eastern Germany had been separated from the rest of the country, it was apparent that Western Germany would not be able to raise enough food stuffs to maintain itself without imports. This was one of the urgent needs that required a strong program of exports of manufactured goods to pay for imports of agricultural products.

The total amount of funds for Technical Assistance was $ 43,606,000 [6]). The largest amount went to Greece, $ 8,179,900, Britain was next with $ 5,314,500, and France with $ 3,397,200. Germany received a relatively small amount, probably because of modest requests and also because Germany had been one of the most progressive manufacturers in Europe. Germany received $ 1,370,200, which was used in exchanges of personnel. ´

The provision for guaranteeing investments by American companies in the countries of Europe did not immediately attract interest, but by the end of the Marshall Plan period $ 37,978,900 was guaranteed to a variety of companies, the largest dealt in chemical products, petroleum refining and machinery with a considerable scattering of other businesses [7]). There were some cancellations and some reductions in value, but this was the beginning of American interest in European plants, which later developed to a considerable degree.

Expenditures by ECA/MSA for freight subsidies on voluntary relief supplies and parcel post packages during the period from 1 July 1948 to 30 June 1952 amounted to $ 25,237,800, of this amount $ 11,308,800 subsidized the shipment to Germany of 399,407,000 pounds of packages directed to Germany; 189,875,000 pounds were sent by voluntary agen-

Summary of Procurement Authorized and Paid Shipments, by Commodity Groups

Commodity or Service	Total	Federal Republic of Germany	France
Grand Total	$ 13,365,400,000	$ 1,389,000,000	$ 2,706,300,000
Commodity Total	11,684,200,000	1,271,800,000	2,330,800,000
Food & Agricultural Items	5,539,700,000	979,200,000	707,000,000
Industrial Commodities	6,167,000,000	296,300,000	1,627,600,000
Unclassified Commodities	− 22,500,000	− 3,700,000	− 3,800,000
Technical Services	60,900,000	2,000,000	14,900,000
Ship Disbursements	9,100,000	200,000	2,000,000
Assistance by E.P.U.	277,800,000	—	—
European Payments Union–Capital	361,400,000	—	—
General Freight Accounts	33,500,000	—	—
Ocean Freight	938,500,000	114,900,000	358,600,000

(Adapted from Table C-4, page 8, Mutual Security Program, Report to Congress, Dec. 1952)

ECA/MSA Approvals of Withdrawals of European Counterpart Funds Available for Use by the Country of Deposit, According to Purpose and Country — 3 April 1948 to 30 June 1952
(Dollar equivalents of local currencies in millions of dollars)

Country		Promotion of Production					
	Total	Electric Gas etc.	Trans. & Comm.	Agric.	Mfg.	Mining	Other
Total	$ 4,466.3	$ 1,025.5	$ 957.5	$ 817.6	$ 681.7	$ 481.8	$ 502.2
Germany	1,753.7	182.6	86.8	70.7	218.7	91.8	103.1
France	1,925.6	738.4	294.2	234.1	249.1	340.6	69.1
Britain	2.2	—	—	.2	—	—	2.0

(continuation)

Country	Monetary Stabilization	Housing & Public Bldgs.	MSA Const.	Other	Total Approved For Withdrawal
Total	$ 2,583.3	$ 767.5	$ 460.9	$ 373.3	$ 8,651.3
Germany	—	97.7	—	157.7	1,009.1
France	171.4	314.4	283.9	7.5	2,702.8
Britain	1,706.7	—	47.5	6.4	1,762.8

(Adapted from Table C-12, page 13, Mutual Security Program, Report to Congress, December 1952)

cies, 201,572,000 pounds came by parcel post [8]). As we have noted previously, this was a substantial aid in providing for the German people who had no resources and were compelled to depend on help from people abroad.

Counterpart Funds

The table containing only the items pertaining to the major countries and the over-all total indicates the uses made of counterpart funds by the major nations. Germany used most of its special assets to rehabilitate the industrial plant, transportation and communication. A considerable amount went into assistance to Berlin. None of it went to pay debts; in fact, any debt that the Hitler government had was repudiated. On the other hand, Britain used almost all its counterpart funds to pay government debts; France used some of its funds for debt payment but concentrated most of its assistance through the counterpart funds on rebuilding its economy. Further consideration of the use of counterpart funds will be taken up in the next chapter.

Industrial Production Index

The economic indicators of industrial production for Western Europe using 1948 as 100, show clearly the progress of Western Europe and the various countries in it.

Industrial Production Indexes for Western Europe 1938, 1949—52
(1948 = 100)

Country	1938	1949	1950	1951	1952
TOTAL	100	113	125	137	138
Belgium	82	100	102	117	114
France	90	110	111	125	134
Germany	193	144	182	218	228
Italy	101	110	126	144	146
Netherlands	88	112	123	129	128
United Kingdom	83	107	116	120	114

(Adapted from Table F-1, page 24, Mutual Security Program, Report to Congress, December 1952)

In taking 1948 for the base of comparison it does not show the progress made by those countries that devoted themselves to getting back to normal quickly after the war. But whether the bases reflect pre-war conditions or those immediately following the war, they all indicate a steady growth in economic activity. Germany, of course, shows the phenomenal activity of the pre-war days in preparing for the war with an index of 193 in 1938; yet the actual growth in the last two years of the Marshall Plan demonstrates clearly the progress that nation had been making.

Foreign Trade

The Combined Foreign Trade of the OEEC Countries — Indexes of Volume and Monthly Averages of Value

Period	Volume	of Trade —	1948 = 100	Value of Trade, Monthly Average in millions of U. S. dollars equiv.		
	Intra-ERP	Imports from Rest of World	Exports to Rest of World	Total Imports	Total Exports	Intra-ERP
1938	136	116	107	$ 1,022	762	384
1948	100	100	100	2,052	1,403	633
1949	124	104	118	2,070	1,569	721
1950	173	100	144	2,018	1,645	811
1951	189	112	169	2,782	2,266	1,061
1952 (2nd Qtr)	175	109	157	2,720	2,207	1,041

(Adapted from Table F-8, p. 27, Mutual Security Program, Report to Congress, December 1952)

This shows a good record, although the imports from the Western Hemisphere are not shown in this table. Those are consistently below the exports to that area with a resulting trade balance against the ERP countries. This was to be expected with the heavy imports from the United States which were necessary to equip and set up the industrial system of the countries which were participants.

It was Representative Mike Mansfield from Montana, now Majority Leader of the Senate, who pointed out that the Marshall Plan had enabled Europe to increase production to $ 30,000,000,000 since 1947, much of the progress in a little more than two and one-half years, whereas, it took seven years after World War I for Europe to reach its pre-war production. In 1938, the ECA countries spent $ 114,000,000,000 for consumer goods; yet in 1949, the same nations spent $ 115,000,000,000 of their increased gross income for consumer products. Most of their added income has gone into capital investment. ECA had made it possible to feed people and to provide tools and jobs for economic independence. ECA had placed a new emphasis on the integration of Europe providing a freer flow of goods in a single market of 260,000,000 people [9]).

History will record that the Marshall Plan was the most effective means 'of setting Europe on the road to economic recovery. It was a costly operation but it changed the attitude of Europeans from looking for charity to working out their own salvation. Although the original estimate of the CEEC was $ 40,000,000,000 to rehabilitate Europe; and Congress cut that down to $ 17,000,000,000 as an estimate, the actual cost of the Marshall Plan was only a little more than $ 12,000,000,000, proof enough that when people try to help themselves it pays to assist them.

[1]) cf. p. 4, The Military Security Program, First Report to Congress, 31 December 1951, U. S. Government Printing Office.

[2]) cf. p. 21, Recovery under the Marshall Plan, 1948—1952; Twelfth, Final Report of the German Federal Government on the Progress of the Marshall Plan for the period until June 30, 1952, by the Federal Minister for the Marshall Plan, Bonn 1953.

[3]) cf. p. 14, Table 14, MSA approvals for withdrawal of European Counterpart Funds available for use — 1 July 1951 to 30 June 1952.

[4]) cf. p. 27, Table F-8, Combined Foreign Trade of OEEC countries, indexes of volume and monthly averages of value, 1938 & 1948—1952, Mutual Security Agency.

[5]) op. cit. p. 27, Table F-9, Combined Foreign Trade of OEEC countries, monthly average in millions of dollars.

[6]) op. cit. p. 10, Table C-5 — Technical Assistance Authorized & Expenditures 3 April 1948 to 30 June 1952.

[7]) op. cit. p. 10, Table C-6 — Value of Industrial Guarantees.

[8]) op. cit. p. 12, Table 6—9, MSA Expenditures for Freight Subsidies on Voluntary Relief Supplies, etc. — 1 July 1948 to 30 June 1952.

[9]) 81st Congress, 2nd Session, Jan. to Dec. 1950, Vol. 96, p. 4059 — The Congressional Record.

Chapter VII

SPECIAL ASSETS — THE COUNTERPART FUNDS

The Failure of Charity Aid

Economic aid to Europe following World War II was by no means a simple matter of open-handed assistance. The United States had given vast sums to keep the victims of war on both sides alive. Not only government aid but private charity flowed to Europe in a steady stream; yet for the most part, it was not the kind of help that might put the nations on their feet fast. Outright gifts apparently were not the answers. Since 1945 to 1948 Congress had appropriated $ 25,495,052,923 in loans, grants, and credits to implement international policy including relief, operational funds for international organizations and nations in trouble, yet there was no sign that such help was establishing countries on a sound economic basis to insure recovery [1]. This figure does not include a vast amount of individual aid through churches and societies that made life bearable in Europe. Yet all these gifts had failed to bring recovery. It was apparent that outright gifts were not the answer.

The simple truth of the matter was that Europe was so badly disrupted that no amount of charity or relief could revive her for years to come. National resources had been drained beyond the limit. Colonial trade brought in little since the Japanese occupation during the war. Rebellion was rife in many of the British, French, Dutch and Belgian colonies. The industrial system had been so badly destroyed that it produced salable commodities with difficulty. Raw materials were scarce, manpower was depleted, management was helpless without operating funds and capital. None of the countries could produce enough to develop income with which to rebuild and worse yet, their capital funds had been wiped out during the war so that they no longer drew income from foreign investments. With such conditions in 1946—48 it seemed likely that Europe was fast becoming a colony of the United States; for leaders looked to America to solve all their problems with an unceasing flow of emergency funds to relieve a series of crises. Some way had to be found to restore the will to work and rebuild trade rather than begging for funds to keep themselves alive.

Basis of the Marshall Plan

The Marshall Plan provided effective aid: 1) to pay dollars for commodities and service that Europe needed; 2) to require recipients to pay for what they received in their own currency; 3) to provide outright grants for emergency cases without disrupting the regular trade; 4) to use accumulated funds of local currencies to promote recovery under some control. The basic idea of the European Recovery Program was ingenious and effective, for it was built on the principle of helping those who were willing to help themselves. Yet even the most efficient system would still require inventive genius to develop; 1) the intra-European payments plan to handle European trade; 2) to insure free movement of materials needed by all, such as coal, iron and steel, fertilizers, etc.; 3) to devise credit arrangements for exports and imports; 4) to open markets to trade without discrimination; and 5) to provide freedom of transportation and communication.

The European Recovery Program, or the Marshall Plan as it came to be known, was built on these ideas. The President's Committee on Foreign Aid stated simply, "We believe that the future of Western Europe lies very much in its own hands. No amount of outside aid, however generous, can by itself restore the health of the economies of the 16 nations which met in Paris in July... The success of any aid program depends ultimately on hard work and straight thinking by the people and the governments of the European nations themselves" [2]). The fact that the European Recovery Program worked at all was the direct result of the planning and efforts of the participating nations, for they determined what would be required to re-establish European economies and what would be required of the people of Europe to make the program work.

A Four-Year Program

The Marshall Plan was a four-year plan, but appropriations were for a single year as required by developing conditions. The Committee of the 16 nations — CEEC as it was called — estimated the needs at an extravagant $ 40,000,000,000 which the President's Committee cut down to $ 17,000,000,000. Developments, however, reduced the amount so that the final total amount of aid was just a little over $ 13,908,900,000, over the four-year period, not including the military subsidy of the MSA. This amount was kept within bounds by the participating nations' committee itself. In the case of two countries, Britain and Ireland, they actually did forego an allotment in the last year because they felt they had recovered enough not to need it.

Payment in Dollars

The first essential feature of the ERP was the payment of dollars by the United States for commodities and services desired by the various nations. This insured reimbursement of the seller in a viable currency that was readily accepted. It gave the buyer what he felt he needed and wanted. It put a premium upon the orders that came through the office of ECA. Much of the materials supplied came from the United States but Canada, Latin American states and Asian countries were also involved.

Payment in Local Currency — Counterpart Funds

The second essential feature, and perhaps the key to the whole program, was the payment by the purchaser for the cost, the insurance and the freight (cif) for delivery in the various European countries, in the currency of his nation to a designated bank account for this purpose. These were called Special Assets, or blocked accounts. The Special Accounts were under government control and not subject to withdrawal except after approval by the ECA Administrator. Moreover, the Special Account funds were divided between the ECA and the country of deposit. 5 % of the total was set aside for the United States to cover the administrative expense of the ERP, the purchase of scarce strategic materials and other uses for United States purposes. The remaining 95 % was strictly for the use of the nation receiving the assistance and was to be used for the purpose of: 1) Expenditures upon projects or programs which are legitimate parts of the development of the productive capacity of the country; 2) Expenditures for the exploration and development of new sources of wealth; 3) Expenditures to retire debt especially that held by banks, but at no time for the current budget; 4) Expenditures to pay transportation charges on private American relief supplies and packages to the port of entry; 5) Expenditures for emergency relief such as Berlin, miners' housing and similar projects. Proposals describing the project as appropriate to the above objectives were submitted to the ECA Administrator and with his approval, withdrawal of the money was authorized.

Purchase not Gifts

This payment in local currencies as the key feature of the Marshall Plan moved the procurement of commodities and services out of the sphere of charity and into the realm of a business. The recipient did not get something for nothing; he paid for it in his own money; and he could look upon it as a straightforward business deal. Furthermore, since he had paid for it in his own money, he valued what he received far more than if it had been given to him. The Marshall Plan had none of the stigma of charity as so many previous funds carried.

Although there were a few exceptions, by far the most of the ERP funds and their counterparts were handled with integrity and justice. Too often in the previous years when materials were shipped into a country they were political largesse, to be meeted out to friends or cronies, or to be sold for private gain of the office holder. Such practices prejudiced people against the management of relief funds and also against the supplies that came. Immediately after the war, the people of several countries who were close to starvation complained bitterly against the distribution of cornmeal instead of wheat flour. Such complaints in ERP were few. Without doubt, instances did occur where Marshall Plan supplies were not administered with efficiency, but they were not frequent and for the most part the operations were well handled.

Cooperation with Banks

Many governments worked with banks in making grants or loans. Here and there a central bank managed all the work but there were also cases, like Germany, where these funds were administered by five banks and seven government departments. The whole operation of the Marshall Plan program was put in the hands of a cabinet minister and at the beginning that minister was also a deputy chancellor, so that these funds and their administration had top priority in the Federal Republic. The German policy of loaning funds from the Special Accounts insisted on sound practice of insuring repayment of principal and the regular payment of interest. A relatively small percentage of the total counterpart fund was authorized as an outright subsidy as was the case in some other countries; therefore, the normal increase of capital loans, subject to amortization and interest payments, was greater in Germany than elsewhere.

GARIOA

The initial aid funds for Germany were known as Government and Relief in Occupied Areas — GARIOA, was not a part of the Marshall Plan but it did provide the start for stimulating economic aid. These funds were provided by Congress for use by the U.S. Army and were designated primarily for food, feed, seeds, fertilizers and medical supplies and fuel. German importers paid for these commodities to special accounts, called DM counterpart accounts with the Bank Deutscher Laender. These were available to finance investments important to the national economy after release by the United States officials. The yearly amounts made available were: 1946—47, $ 263,080,000; 1947—48, $ 580,190,000; 1948—49, $ 578,550,000 and 1949—50, $ 198,380,000 making a total of $ 1,620,200,000. On March 31, 1950, the unspent GARIOA funds were transferred to the ECA funds and this organization completed the administration of the outstanding grants. These were used largely for relief purposes and it was understood that the full amount would not be repaid. On June 30, 1951, in the context of the London Conference on Debt Settlement, the West German Government signed an agreement with the United States to repay about one-third of this total amount in 35 annual payments to the United States. The actual commodity distribution of the GARIOA Fund was: Food stuffs $ 1,172,880,000; fertilizers and seeds $ 104,850,000; fuel $ 69,800,000; medical supplies $ 60,000; transportation of goods $ 186,830,000; salaries of civilian staff $ 65,170,000 and the remainder, $ 13,682,000 for such items as informational and educational services, exchange programs, travel, etc. [3]).

Total Counterpart Funds from 1948—1952

The total amount of expenditures under the Marshall Plan requiring counterpart deposits was $ 10,826,000,000; the actual deposits amounted to $ 10,509,800,000. The adjusted dollar equivalents of the deposits, less the adjustments due to currency devaluation in 1951 was $ 9,829,400,000. Deposits made under other public laws 84 and 389, subject to ECA/MSA approval, was $ 597,500,000. The total available for the countries' use was $ 9,952,300,000, of which $ 8,651,300,000 was approved for withdrawal and $ 8,399,080,000 was actually withdrawn. Although this was spread over 16 countries, it was still a substantial sum to be invested in the interests of rebuilding the economic systems of those nations. The following table (page 86) sets forth the distribution among the participating nations, Germany had Marshall Plan funds amounting to $ 1,346,200,000 requiring counterpart deposits. Actual deposits were the same amount. The total available — the 95 % part — for in the country was $ 1,079,200,000 and actual withdrawals were $ 1,008,000,000. Britain and France received more than Germany, $ 2,088,000,000 and $ 2,562,400,000 respectively.

Distribution of Counterpart Funds

The distribution of counterpart funds according to uses is also significant, for of the total $ 8,651,300,000 approved for withdrawal, $ 4,466,300,000 was used for the promotion of production, $ 2,583,300,000 for monetary and financial stabilization; $ 767,500,000 for housing and public buildings; and $ 460,900,000 for military construction, production and procurement under the MSA program. Since rehabilitation of production and housing are closely related, it is evident that almost two-thirds of the total went into the primary objective activity of the Marshall Plan. The following table (page 87) indicates the expenditures of the approval ERP counterpart funds.

The variety of uses of the Marshall Plan counterpart funds inevitably reflected the particular problems and goals of the countries themselves. The traditional industries of the different peoples required rehabilitation, but many of them looked for new production which would develop their commercial life. OEEC faced the expected conflict of interests at this point, for it could not encourage countries to enter a new field for their

Status of European Local Currency Counterpart Accounts [4]) *by Country,*
Cumulative, 3 April 1948 to 30 June 1952

(Dollar equivalents of local currency in millions of dollars)

Country	ECA/MSA Expenditure requiring deposit	Adjusted dollar equivalents to currency change							
		Deposits	Total	Reserved for use by U.S.	Available for use by recipient country	Deposits under other public laws	Total available — country use	Approved with- drawals	With- drawals
Total	10,826.0	10,599.8	9,829.4	474.6	9,354.8	579.5	9,952.3	8,651.3	8,399.08
Austria	871.8	847.1	699.6	32.1	667.5	112.1	779.6	527.3	526.7
Belgium-Luxembourg	25.6	25.9	25.5	1.5	24.0	—	24.0	3.8	2.3
Denmark	257.3	257.3	225.1	11.3	213.8	—	213.8	204.1	118.9
France	2,562.4	2,533.2	2,508.2	112.8	2,395.4	308.9	2,704.3	2,702.8	2,702.6
Germany	1,346.2	1,346.2	1,140.0	60.8	1,079.2	—	1,079.2	1,009.1	1,008.0
Greece	905.5	893.8	847.2	40.5	806.2	3.0	809.7	361.1	361.1
Iceland	20.9	20.4	19.0	1.0	18.0	—	18.0	5.8	5.8
Ireland	18.2	18.2	18.2	.9	17.3	—	17.3	—	—
Italy	1,059.1	1,040.8	1,010.3	51.3	959.0	173.2	1,132.2	1,042.4	1,026.8
Netherlands	902.5	880.0	815.9	40.0	775.9	—	775.9	547.6	505.7
Indonesia	114.9	114.9	48.2	4.8	43.4	—	43.4	—	—
Norway	365.6	364.9	351.3	16.6	334.7	—	334.7	301.1	200.9
Portugal	21.2	21.2	20.6	1.2	19.4	—	19.4	18.4	18.4
Trieste	36.7	36.1	35.6	1.8	33.8	.3	34.1	32.3	31.2
Turkey	143.7	134.4	134.4	6.0	128.4	—	128.4	128.4	128.4
United Kingdom	2,088.0	1,983.9	1,890.9	90.0	1,800.9	—	1,800.9	1,762.8	1,762.8
Yugoslavia	86.9	73.5	39.4	2.0	37.4	—	37.4	4.3	—

MSA/ECA Approvals for Withdrawal of European Counterpart Funds Available for Country Use by Purpose and Country, Cumulative, 3 April 1948 — 30 June 1952
(Dollar equivalents of local curencies, in millions of dollars)

Country	Total	Purpose of Approval — Promotion of Production					
		Electric Gas & Other Power	Transportation & Communication	Agriculture	Manufacturing	Mining	Other Production
TOTAL	$4,466.3	$1,025.5	$957.5	$817.6	$681.7	$481.8	$502.2
Denmark	62.4	.6	2.8	11.2	6.7	—	41.1
France	1,925.6	738.4	294.2	234.1	249.2	340.6	69.1
Germany	753.7	182.6	86.8	70.7	218.7	91.8	103.1
Italy	823.8	1.0	348.9	204.8	22.6	—	246.5
Netherlands	212.8	—	13.6	166.5	32.3	—	.4
Norway	8.4	—	2.7	—	—	5.7	—
Turkey	51.0	.6	13.9	15.2	8.0	14.7	4.6
United Kingdom	2.2	—	—	.2	—	—	2.0

Continued

Country	Monetary and Financial Stability	Housing & Public Buildings	Military Construction Production % Procurement	Other	Total Approved for Withdrawal
TOTAL	$2,583.3	$767.5	$460.9	$373.3	$8,651.3
Denmark	130.1	—	9.4	2.2	204.1
France	171.4	314.4	283.9	7.5	2,702.8
Germany	—	97.7	—	157.7	1,009.1
Italy	—	172.7	—	45.9	1,042.4
Netherlands	197.4	88.1	46.3	3.0	547.6
Norway	292.7	—	—	—	301.1
Turkey	—	—	60.4	11.0	128.4
United Kingdom	1,706.7	—	47.5	6.4	1,762.8

Adapted from Table C-12, p. 13, Report to Congress, Mutual Security Agency, Dec. 1952 (Seven smaller countries' approvals not shown)

own economic system and set up unreasonable competition for those which had been working in those fields. In some cases, nations undertook to enter fields where the German firms had been prominent, but they soon found out that the established German skills, trained workers, and knowledge of their markets gave the German industries an important advantage. Natural resources played an important part. As we have noted some of the countries used their counterpart funds to pay off national debts with the hope of strengthening their stability. Denmark used $ 130,100,000 for that purpose, as did France $ 171,400,000, the Netherlands to the amount of $ 197,400,000, and Britain $ 1,706,400,000. Such payments had an immediate benefit, but did not strengthen the economic life by a new infusion of capital. The benefit of new capital investment was evident in most countries. The major investments were made in 1) Electric power plants to meet new demands; 2) Transport and communication rehabilitation and extension; 3) Agriculture which was an urgent need in almost all countries; 4) Mining which absorbed $ 481,800,000 and other manufacturing and production which used more than $ 1,183,900,000 and 5) Housing and public building rehabilitation and extension $ 767,500,000.

West Germany's Problems

As we have already noted, the West German Republic had the most serious problems in recovering from the war. The destruction of cities, transportation, and human life was by far the most serious in Central Europe. It also had the burden of military occupation, the division of its territory and the resulting disruption of its traditional industrial and commercial system. The people of Germany needed more help because of the war damage and they had the least possible chance of assistance because of the bitterness developed by the war. The first two or three years of military occupation were almost paralysis of life itself, and recovery from such inertia was particularly difficult. For many people there seemed no possible chance of rebuilding the economic life of the country, and many former leaders saw no chance of re-establishing themselves.

In spite of this combination of negative factors, the re-organizing of the country's political life-first the towns and cities, then the Laender, and finally the Federal Republic—stirred the spirit of enough people to start a revival of hope. Although industrial and commercial activity seemed hopelessly stalled, the efforts of the other European countries which were participants in the European Recovery Program revived their spirits. Then, too, the efforts of civilian officers of Military Government, especially in the American Zone gave them help in rebuilding national life. The proud Germany harbored a secret admiration for the American Military Government and its personnel and led them to dream of reviving their nation with some of the potential capabilities of their people developing along the lines of the American people. In the years following the war, American leaders were asked again and again what was the secret of American power and might. Because the United States had come to be a dominant power, it was natural for the defeated to look to the victor as a pattern of achievement and success.

Germany's Participation in OEEC

Immediately after the establishment of the Federal Republic and Germany's admission to the OEEC as a full member, this step took on a challenge to Germans because it was their first chance to work on an equal footing with the leaders of other nations, most of whom had been their enemies during the war. The wise choice of leadership for the Marshall Plan and the sound policies that were adopted in using these funds laid the foundation of a reconstruction of the German physical plant and also the spirit of the people. Chancellor Adenauer's action in creating a cabinet post for the administrator of the Marshall Plan operation set the standard for all to take full advantage of the opportunity. This ERP program became a major factor in opening the way to further cooperation between the German leaders and the other Western European political officials. German technicians were given responsible places in the OEEC and when the High Authority for Coal and Steel was set up, the choice of officers of high calibre inevitably led to some of the Germans as well as other Europeans. Chancellor Adenauer's continual emphasis on Germany as a unit of a new European entity — Europa — gave his people the avenue to a new understanding of their place in the world.

The German Management of Counterpart Funds

The Adenauer administration saw in the counterpart funds a most needed reserve for capital investment and this fund was administered toward the goal of reviving German native ability and the will to work. While the counterpart funds amounted to only $ 1,079,200,000, it was immediately available for investment and carefully husbanded, it could grow into a sizable amount to strengthen German industrial resources. The policies and practices adopted by the Bundestag and the Cabinet wisely conserved the funds they had so that over the years they grew to a substantial source of capital to develop German resources. By 1967, this fund, through careful management, had become somewhat more than 21,350,000,000 DM or $ 5,337,500,000 and in its management had touched almost every phase 'of German life. In recent years, it has also furnished the funds for substantial aid to the developing countries of Asia and Africa.

The table below (page 91) shows the extent of the use of these funds in the four years of the Marshall Plan.

Some particular items are worthy of special mention, such as the use of the counterpart funds to expand the coal mining industry upon which European industry depended. This was accomplished by: 1) systematizing and mechanizing the collieries, especially at the coal face; 2) increasing output; and 3) providing housing for the miners and their families. More than 726,000,000 DM from the counterpart funds was allocated for this project. Nine major housing projects of 600—800 units located in suitable places and in well-planned towns were devised with a plan of eventual ownership by the occupant.

An urgently needed power station program to build 67 new plants, producing 2,790 million watts was financed with the aid of the counterpart assets. A total of 1,185,860,000 DM, of which 828,000,000 DM came from ECA and GARIOA funds. These plants supplied 22 % of the power needed by West Germany. For the expansion of the iron and steel industry 167,700,000 DM was loaned by Special Assets. The financing and purchase of ocean-going ships took 1,528,522,000 DM, of which 301,360,000 was supplied by ECA counterpart funds.

Agriculture Funds
Credits for agriculture, including food processing, in Western Germany drew heavily upon the counterpart funds; GARIOA 1949 provided

Programs in Federal Territory Financed Through Funds from the Special Assets Counterpart Funds, as of 31 December 1952
(in million DM)

Branches of Economy	Prior to 15/12/1949		ERP Issues Branches of			ERP Interest and Amortization	TOTAL
	ECA	GARIOA	1950 I	1951 II	1952 III		
Electric Power	58.5	110.0	220.7	134.5	356.3	87.5	987.3
Gas & Water	.5	—	35.6	35.4	15.	23.1	109.6
Coal Mining	50.	135.	150.	116.	130.	—	581.
Steel Industry	—	—	37.9	54.8	75.	—	167.7
Export Industry	—	—	—	—	46.7	—	46.7
Other Industries	—	5.	233.4	199.2	—	70.5	518.1
Crafts & Small Trade	—	—	—	0.2	—	20.	20.2
Agriculture	—	—	121.5	111.3	140.	22.3	395.1
Federal Railways	40.	360	—	20.	45.	10.	455.
Federal Post	—	—	—	20.	—	—	20.
Grants for Agriculture	—	—	—	73.6	39.9	—	113.5
Housing Construction	—	—	81.5	115.3	280.	—	476.8
Shipping	—	—	50.	36.2	85.	31.9	203.1
Fishing Trawlers	—	5.0	—	—	—	—	5.0
Inland Shipping	—	—	—	9.4	—	5.	14.4
Inland Ports	2.0	—	—	9.9	—	—	11.9
Tramways	—	—	7.0	10.3	—	.3	17.6
Private R.Rs.	—	—	—	6.7	—	—	6.7
Seaports	—	—	—	4.7	—	—	4.7
Transport Enterprise	—	—	—	0.7	—	—	0.7
Tourist Trade	—	—	—	22.6	—	5.2	27.8
Expellee Enterprise	—	—	—	70.5	25.—	25.—	120.5
Research	—	—	—	20.9	9.9	4.0	34.8
Export Promotion	—	—	—	2.3	2.0	—	4.3
Special Zonal Front	—	—	—	—	—	6.0	6.0
TOTAL	151.	625.	937.6	1,054.3	1,249.8	310.8	4,326.5

(Adapted from p. 29, Recovery under the Marshall Plan, 1948—1952, The Federal Minister for the Marshall Plan, 1953)

5,000,000 DM; ERP-I—1950, 121,500,000 DM; ERP-II—1951, 11,300,000 DM; ERP-III—1952, 140,000,000 DM; interest and amortization to 1952, 22,300,000 DM and West Berlin aid funds 1,400,000 DM; along with 113,500,000 DM of unrecoverable grants. The table below gives the details of the uses of the agricultural credits:

Utilization of Agricultural Credits (including West Berlin) from ERP Special Assets [5]) (as of 31 December 1952)

OBJECT	in 1000 DM	Percent of Total Amount
Reconstruction of destroyed buildings	47,810	11.8 %
Soil Improvement (water economy, land consolidation, and deforestation)	64,066	15.8
Refugee Settlement on farms	42,744	10.7
Inventory credits excluding machinery	26,860	6.7
Machinery	57,891	14.3
Fruit and Vegetable Storage	1,800	0.4
Fruit and Vegetable Marketing	4,000	1.0
Marketing of Miscellaneous products	2,280	0.6
Fishing excluding fish industry	5,700	1.4
Sugar Production	34,250	8.5
Dairies	21,594	5.3
Expansion & Improvement of pastures & Fodder	16,500	4.1
Food Processing Industries	21,281	5.3
Miscellaneous Production for distressed areas	50,000	12.4
West Berlin Agriculture & Food Supply	4,280	1.1
Miscellaneous projects	3,000	0.6
TOTAL	404,056	100.—

Typical of the policy planning for the future was the action of the Minister for the Marshall Plan who set aside the interest on two agricultural credit programs totaling 90,000,000 DM to insure the continuation of the Agricultural Advisory and Information Service started with the help of the American Department of Agriculture.

The 33,000,000 DM used to subsidize the settlement of refugees on vacant farms made it possible to take over 35,000 farms. 25,000,000 DM came from ERP counterpart funds and more than 8,000,000 DM from amortization and interest. To this was added funds appropriated by the Federal Republic and the various Laender. Setting up refugees in trades or businesses of their own used 92,500,000 DM from the counterpart funds and these became valuable additions to the economy, many of them brought by refugees from the Eastern Zone.

Industrial Funds

The record shows that in industry 81.4 % of the recipients received 86.6 % of the amount of counterpart funds; in trade 6.2 % of the recipients received 4.3 % of the amounts; and in other businesses 12.4 % of the recipients received 9.1 % of the amounts [6]). Of industry's part, only one-seventh of the loans went to new industries. Aid to industry often carried with it an obligation to employ and train expellees and refugees. Wisely the Ministry required that 25 % of the loans be used for operating capital and in the case of the expellee industries, the figure was 8.4 % to enable them to make greater use of their funds. Most of such grants were handled by the Equalization of Burdens Bank with capital funds from Special Assets in the amount of 3,000,000 DM to launch the institutions.

Credits for housing followed a similar pattern. More than 11 % of all the German counterpart funds were used on housing construction. Although the ERP Special Assets Funds were regarded only as complementary in financing of construction, they did provide at least 125,000 dwellings.

The table below indicates the details:

Utilization of Counterpart Funds for Housing Construction

OBJECT	in millions DM
Public housing construction in general	203.90
Expellee housing — Schleswig Holstein	40.00
Lower Saxony	30.00
Bavaria	20.90
Development projects (65 % for expellees)	37.00
Miners' housing — through diversion of coal credits	23.67
program I	45.00
program II	100.00
TOTAL	500.47

(Adapted from p. 33, Recovery under the Marshall Plan, 1948—1952, The Federal Minister for the Marshall Plan, 1953)

In addition to providing funds the Ministry insisted that in the housing construction modern developments be used such as: location in key building sites, standardization of components, special instruction on building particularly suitable housing and the use of the most economical materials locally or from a central supply. These standards were strictly enforced so that Germany today has the most modern construction and planning for living quarters, at lower prices, encouraging better living. While no set patterns were applied, contests were held and prizes awarded for new and improved housing. Special Assets Funds were used where other funds were reluctant to finance a new idea. In 1950, there were almost no second mortgage funds for loans and the counterpart funds took the place of this need.

Technical Assistance

Technical assistance carried on with the aid of counterpart funds was a growing program. A limited amount of personnel exchange was undertaken in the early years of 1947 and 1948, but with additional funds it was expanded. German leaders in all fields from education to business had been cut off from contact with the rest of the world during the Hitler regime. They were well aware that they were out of touch with progress outside Germany. They welcomed the chance to visit other countries and they were pleased to have experts and technicians visit Germany.

Of course, the authorizations from major appropriations of the Marshall Plan funds provided most of the technical assistance. The total amount for the four-year period was $ 43,606,000, with total expenditures of $ 24,993,000; the cost of the program was $ 4,190,700 for administration. $ 10,181,800 was spent for industrial productivity; $ 4,288,500 for agricultural productivity; $ 2,140,700 for Public Administration; $ 1,985,400 for transportation and communications; $ 1,345,200 for manpower utilization; $ 440,400 for marketing; $ 275,700 for development of overseas territories; and $ 144,600 for tourism. From counterpart funds, the total amount programmed for technical assistance was 1,500,000,000 DM [7]). The Germans were particularly systematic in spreading the benefits of visits to foreign lands. Those who were thus privileged, spent much time in writing and speaking to associates in their own occupations. The government officials also drew heavily on the practices established in the United States government, particularly the Office of Technical Services of the Department of Commerce and the Bureau of Labor Statistics. Many of the most modern ideas in manufacturing, packing and shipping, as well as marketing, were taken up eagerly by the Germans who visited other countries and who entertained visiting experts from foreign lands. The rapid absorption of American technology especially was a large factor in the rapid growth of economic progress in Germany.

Thanks-in-Kind

One of the very encouraging developments which grew out of the Marshall Plan has been a more recent program undertaken by the German government as an expression of appreciation for what it gained from the ERP. Since 1960, a formal program of assistance to emerging nations has been developed by the German government. A center for training officials of these nations was set up in Berlin and the year-round programs of training-on-the-job had gone forward with enthusiasm and wisdom. Some projects for development of the economies of these nations have been undertaken. Up to 31 December 1967, the amount of 2,202,915,607 DM has been invested in this effort. It is a demonstration of passing on what one has found valuable in received aid from others. This labor of humanity is, perhaps, the most poignant way of thanking the United States for its aid in times of trouble.

[1]) Reported by Rep. Rich of Pennsylvania, page 1405 of the Congressional Record of the 81st Congress, First Session, June to October, 1949.
[2]) See Chapter I, page 10.
[3]) p. 24, Recovery under the Marshall Plan, 1948—1952, The Federal Minister for the Marshall Plan, Bonn 1953.
[4]) cf. p. 13, Table C-11, Report to Congress, Mutual Security Agency, December 1953.
[5]) cf. p. 31, Recovery under the Marshall Plan, 1948—1952, The Federal Minister for the Marshall Plan, 1953.
[6]) p. 32, Recovery under the Marshall Plan, 1948—1952, The Federal Minister for the Marshall Plan, 1953.
[7]) p. 9, Table C-5, Technical Assistance Authorizations & Expenditures 3 April 1948 to 30 June 1952, Report to Congress, Mutual Security Agency, December 1953.

Chapter VIII

CONCLUSION

The Miracle of German Recovery

Like all economic miracles the German Wirtschaftswunder was the result
of wise planning, hard work and well-timed aid. With all due credit to
the German leaders and their people, the German recovery could not have
been accomplished alone; it was part and parcel of European recovery for
Germany is an essential unit of Europe. The frenetic efforts to keep a
war-weary and broken people alive was an integral part of World War II,
and its aftermath. Yet all the relief and emergency aid had not put Europe
back on its feet. Moreover, relief would never have revived the defeated
and destroyed Germany. The series of relief efforts following the war
soon proved that. As always, the American people could not allow people,
even enemy people, to live in misery and to die from want of food and
medical help. So the years passed with the new attempts to start Europe
again and again, but progress was negligible. We have already noted that
the United States had given more than $ 25,500,000,000 in various forms of
relief from 1945 to 1948 with no prospect of ending the demands for help.

Each nation had turned from war to peace-time pursuits immediately
after 1945, with the hope that life could be taken up where it had been
broken off. Most of the countries showed some immediate improvement,
as the repair of war damage went forward. Britain had a brief surge of
export trading but it dropped off soon. Other nations did not even have
that much of a lift. Some, like Switzerland and Sweden who had not been
immediately involved in the fighting, showed gains in their economic
activities. But all were plagued by financial troubles growing out of the
war and its long waste of material and human resources. No matter
how hard the individual nations seemed to work, they did not make
progress. So again and again, they turned to the United States for emergency help. This could not go on indefinitely, and Secretary George
C. Marshall insisted, in his Harvard address in June 1947, that a new

and effective way to help get Europe started economically was urgently needed.

Looking back now, the answer to the problem does not seem difficult in the light of what happened, but statesmen were not solving the matter. The simple fact was that Europe without Germany could not rebuild effectively and Germany without Europe could not do so either. All Europe needed coal that Germany had in the mines, without it modern industry did not function. Moreover, the natural resources of Europe were too scattered and without some integration the economy of the continent could not be revived quickly. If a nation tried to trade with another there were tariffs and customs to impede them. In fact, all European countries were dependent upon others in some way. Europe had never learned that only when it was united, even under an emperor or dictator, did it prosper and grow. Yet each time the vast holdings of an imperialist broke up, Europe went into decline. Even today, there are many politicians with extreme nationalist beliefs who stand in the way of a United Europe in which the people of all Europe can enjoy the resources of all Europe.

The Key to American Aid

Although Secretary Marshall did not point out this fact, he did stress the need for Europe to study its own problems and to work out some practical solution for reviving the economic life of this region. He went further to say that the United States would provide assistance for those who would help themselves. This brought about the meeting of Britain, France and the Soviet Union, but the Soviets would not agree to help rebuild Europe. Another attempt was made by the Committee of European Economic Cooperation, composed of representatives of sixteen nations, and they produced a plan to submit to the United States. President Truman appointed a Committee on Foreign Aid to Europe to which the proposal was referred and the recommendations of that group were influential in convincing the American Congress that a new plan for help might be successful and the Foreign Aid Bill was passed. This authorized the year by year appropriation of aid to be administered by the Economic Cooperation Administration. We have already noted that the essential features of this Program were: 1) Yearly appropriation of needed funds for specific purposes; 2) Dollar payments, by the United States, for commodities and services; and 3) Payment of counterpart funds in the currency of the country receiving the goods which could be used only with the consent of the American Administrator for specific objectives as set forth in requests for loans or grants. Thus, in effect, the United States gave European nations double the sum of the American aid. By rigorous administration, the resources of this Program were not squandered in political mismanagement as were many previous aid funds. The whole Program was directed by the Organization for European Economic Cooperation (OEEC) working with the American Economic Cooperation Administration staff (ECA). The results were prompt and effective. While the first years required much food for sheer maintenance, in the later periods the funds went to rebuilding the productive machinery of the nations and getting the raw materials to manufacture. In the four years of the program, really three, because this European Recovery Program was telescoped into the Mutual Security Agency to equip and organize NATO in 1951, the changes wrought in Europe were prodigious.

Total Aid and Counterpart Funds

The record shows that the United States paid out $ 13,365,400,000 for commodities requested by the sixteen participating nations of the European Recovery Program. $ 5,539,700,000 went for food and agricultural commodities and $ 6,167,000,000 for industrial commodities and $ 1,658,700,000 for other services, freight, etc. This not only fed Europe but it provided the industrial system's rehabilitation and expansion. To this must be added the total counterpart deposits of $ 10,509,800,000, 95 % of which was available for further assistance to participating nations. The Federal Republic of Germany received $ 1,389,000,000 from ECA for various commodities and services and $ 1,346,200,000 in counterpart funds. We have already seen what extensive help these funds served in re-establishing the German industrial system. But the benefits of the Marshall Plan were more than money for commodities. It gave people of Europe and especially Germany a new lease on life with the promise of better times ahead. It substituted work for charity; it stimulated efficient administration of funds and national budgets; it developed a normal and logical export and import trade; and it demonstrated the value of a unified economy in the whole area of Europe.

Germany's Unique Contribution

The unique contribution of Germany was the totally new attitude of the people and the leaders under the stimulating and dynamic personality of Chancellor Konrad Adenauer and the economic genius of Professor Ludwig Erhard. Chancellor Adenauer brought to the task the skill of a professional civil servant who was dedicated to democratic ways, and who frequently said, "We Germans must prove to the world that we can be good neighbors, before we can expect to be accepted". Professor Erhard had the courage to lead in the currency change, and to abolish the government price regulations that were binding West Germany. It was his work as the executive of the Bizonal organization in 1947 and 1948 that laid the foundation on which an economic revival could be built. Above all, the German people were ready to follow such leadership and were willing to work to achieve it.

Germany and the Refugees

In the late months of the war, Germany was burdened with a growing number of refugees and when the war was over the complicated problem of finding food and shelter and jobs for the millions of expellees and refugees took all the inventive genius and work habits to cope with this mounting burden. When the refugees fled into Germany before the retreating army there was little that could be done for them. And when the Czecho-slovak authorities hauled 2,900,000 people to the German border and dumped them on the helpless German civil servants they had no choice but to find a place for them. When later waves of refugees and expellees swept in from the East — the fleeing East Prussians, the Pomeranians, the Upper Silesians, the East Germans and others — the pitiful scene was re-enacted again and again. A defeated people was compelled to take these victims into their homes. While the burden was almost unbearable at the time, later these very unwelcome persons were incorporated into the German life and eventually they became one of the very great assets, without which Germany could never have become the Wirtschaftswunder the world admires today. These victims of expulsion became the workers who manned the rapidly growing German industry and in some cases brought with them new industries for the benefit of the Federal Republic of Germany.

The Proportion of Counterpart Funds

One of the lesser miracles was the way the German savings flowed into industrial investment when the counterpart funds proved that these capital loans were sound. The following table shows how large a part German money was in the revival of capital funds for industry and agriculture. No further evidence is needed to prove that the Marshall Plan funds were important in starting the flow of capital. Once the people saw that ECA funds would be provided to undertake a variety of necessary activities, it was taken as a proof of the integrity of the objective, and German funds emerged to supplement those from abroad. In this respect, the counterpart funds were the starters that "fired the engine of the German economy" as was said in the original President's Committee report.

Aid to Economic Revival

Perhaps the most important contribution of the Federal Republic of Germany was the pre-eminent place that was given to the ECA funds by appointing a minister with cabinet rank, and even a deputy Chancellor to administer the Marshall Plan funds. The policies that were established in the early years of the Federal Republic's history set the high standard of administration that was to characterize its work throughout the years.

The result has been that today the Marshall Plan funds have grown in size and prestige so that any important project that receives partial support from the counterpart funds is immediately accepted as a sound undertaking. Its steady accumulation of interest and capital fund repayment increased the Counterpart Funds or Special Assets from the original amount of $ 1,079,200,000 at the end of 1952 to the present total of $ 5,337,500,000, or 21,350,000,000 DM. Such a growing capital fund available for investment in the expansion of the German economy is a tremendous asset to the thriving industrial system of the nation. In a very definite way, it is a guarantee of the continuing progress of the Federal Republic of Germany as an economic power of first rank.

The Proportionate Sources of Financing Total Imports to the Federal Republic

	Total Imports Million Dollars	%	Food & Agr. Prod. Million Dollars	%	Trade & Industry Million Dollars	%
1949 — Oct.-Dec.						
ECA	$ 99,157,000	15.6	$ 49,333,000	13.8	$ 49,824,000	18.
GARIOA	138,308,000	21.8	125,723,000	35.	12,585,000	4.6
German Funds	397,928,000	62.6	183,649,000	51.2	214,279,000	77.4
	633,393,000	100.	358,705,000	100.	276,688,000	100.
1950 —						
ECA	302,610,000	11.2	119,666,000	10.	182,944,000	12.1
GARIOA	177,800,000	6.6	122,371,000	10.3	55,429,000	3.7
German Funds	2,225,284,000	82.2	950,305,000	79.7	1,272,979,000	84.2
	2,703,694,000	100.	1,192,342,000	100.	1,511,352,000	100.
1951 —						
ECA	415,768,000	11.9	232,075,000	16.6	183,693,000	8.7
GARIOA	11,899,000	.3	5,164,000	.4	6,735,000	.3
German Funds	3,075,333,000	87.8	1,160,248,000	83.0	1,915,085,000	91.0
	3,503,000,000	100.	1,397,487,000	100.	2,105,515,000	100.
1952 —						
ECA	114,098,000	3.0	48,792,000	3.4	65,306,000	2.7
GARIOA	379,000	.0	379,000	.0	—	—
German Funds	3,739,396,000	97.0	1,393,221,000	96.6	2,346,175,000	97.3
	3,853,873,000	100.	1,442,392,000	100.	2,411,481,000	100.
Grand Total	10,695,960,000		4,390,925,000		6,305,034,000	

(Adapted from Table p. 24, Recovery under the Marshall Plan, 1948—1952, The Federal Minister for the Marshall Plan, 1953)

Appendix

ECONOMIC COOPERATION AGREEMENT BETWEEN THE UNITED STATES OF AMERICA AND THE UNITED STATES AND UNITED KINGDOM OCCUPIED AREAS IN GERMANY

PREAMBLE

The Government of the United States of America, and the United States and United Kingdom Military Governors in Germany, acting on behalf of the United States and United Kingdom occupied areas in Germany:

Recognizing that the restoration or maintenance in European countries of principles of individual liberty, free institutions, and genuine independence rests largely upon the establishment of sound economic conditions, stable international economic relationships and the achievement by the countries of Europe of a healthy economy independent of extraordinary outside assistance;

Recognizing that a strong and prosperous European economy is essential for the attainment of the purposes of the United Nations;

Considering that the achievement of such conditions calls for a European Recovery Plan of self-help and mutual cooperation, open to all nations which cooperate in such a plan, based upon a strong production effort, the expansion of foreign trade, the creation or maintenance of internal financial stability and the development of economic cooperation, including all possible steps to establish and maintain valid rates of exchange and to reduce trade barriers;

Considering that in furtherance of these principles the Military Governors, on behalf of the United States/United Kingdom occupied areas, joined with like-minded nations in a convention for European economic cooperation signed at Paris on April 16, 1948, under which the signatories of that convention agreed to undertake as their immediate task the elaboration and execution of a joint recovery program, and that the United States/United Kingdom occupied areas are a member of the organization for European economic cooperation created pursuant to the provisions of that convention;

Considering also that, in furtherance of these principles, the Government of the United States of America has enacted the Economic Cooperation Act of 1948, providing for the furnishing of assistance by the United States of America to nations participating in a joint program for European recovery, in order to enable such nations through their own individual and concerned efforts to become independent of extraordinary outside economic assistance;

Taking note that the Military Governors have already expressed their adherence to the purposes and policies of the Economic Cooperation Act of 1948;

Desiring to set forth the understandings which govern the furnishing of assistance by the Government of the United States of America under the Economic Cooperation Act of 1948, the receipt of such assistance by the United States/United Kingdom occupied areas and the measures which the two parties will take individually and together in furthering the recovery of the United States/United Kingdom occupied areas as an integral part of the joint program for European recovery;

Have agreed as follows:

Article I

(Assistance and Cooperation)

1. The Government of the United States of America undertakes to assist the United States/United Kingdom occupied areas, by making available to the Military Governors or to any person, agency or organization designated by the latter such assistance as may be requested by them and approved by the Government of the United States of America. The Government of the United States of America will furnish this assistance under the provisions, and subject to all the terms, conditions and termination provisions, of the Economic Cooperation Act of 1948, acts amendatory and supplementary thereto and appropriation acts thereunder, and will make available to the Military Governors only such commodities, services and other assistance as are authorized to be made available by such acts.

2. The Military Governors, acting directly and through the Organization for European Economic Cooperation, consistently with the Convention for

European Economic Cooperation signed at Paris on 16 April 1948, will exert sustained efforts in common with other participating countries speedily to achieve through a joint recovery program economic conditions in Europe essential to lasting peace and prosperity and to enable the countries of Europe participating in such a joint recovery program to become independent of extraordinary outside economic assistance within the period of this agreement. The Military Governors reaffirm their intention to take action to carry out the provisions of the General Obligations of the Convention for European Economic Cooperation, to continue to participate actively in the work of the Organization for European Economic Cooperation, and to continue to adhere to the purposes and policies of the Economic Cooperation Act of 1948.

3. All assistance furnished by the Government of the United States of America to the United States/ United Kingdom occupied areas pursuant to this Agreement shall constitute a claim against Germany. To the extent that expenditures are made from the special account established under Article IV of this Agreement for the purposes set forth in paragraphs 3 and 4 of that Article and for purposes not of direct benefit to the German economy, such claim against Germany shall be reduced in an amount commensurate with such expenditures. The proceeds of exports from all future production and stocks of the United States/ United Kingdom occupied areas will be available for payment for assistance made available pursuant to this Agreement. At the earliest practicable time consistent with the rebuilding of the German economy on healthy, non-aggressive lines, such proceeds shall be applied for such payment on a basis at least as favorable to the United States as that accorded the United States for imports made pursuant to the memorandum of agreement between the United States and the United Kingdom dated 2 December 1946, as revised and supplemented, relating to the economic integration of the United States and United Kingdom Zones of Germany.

4. With respect to assistance furnished by the Government of the United States of America to the United States/United Kingdom occupied areas and procured from areas outside the United States of America, its territories and possessions, the Military Governors will cooperate with the Government of the United States of America ensuring that procurement will be effected at reasonable prices and on reasonable terms and so as

to arrange that the dollars thereby made available to the country from which the assistance is procured and used in a manner consistent with any arrangements made by the Government of the United States of America and such country.

Article II

(General Undertaking)

1. In order to achieve the maximum recovery through the employment of assistance received from the Government of the United States of America, the Military Governors will use their best endeavors to assure:

a) the adoption or maintenance of the measures necessary to ensure efficient and practical use of all the resources available to the United States/United Kingdom occupied areas, including

i) such measures as may be necessary to ensure that the commodities and services obtained with assistance furnished under this agreement are used for purposes consistent with this agreement and as far as practicable, with the general purposes outlined in the schedules furnished by the Military Governors in support of the requirements of assistance to be furnished by the Government of the United States of America; and

ii) the observation and review of the use of such resources through an effective follow-up system approved by the Organization for European Economic Cooperation.

b) the promotion of industrial and agricultural production on a sound economic basis along healthy non-aggressive lines; the achievement of such production targets as may be established through the Organization for European Economic Cooperation; and when desired by the Government of the United States of America, the communication to that Government of detailed proposals for specific projects contemplated by the Military Governors to be undertaken in substantial part with assistance made available pursuant to this agreement, including whenever practicable projects for increased production of coal, transportation facilities and food;

105

c) the stabilization of the currency, the establishment and maintenance of a valid rate of exchange, the balancing of the governmental budgets as soon as practicable, the creation or maintenance of internal financial stability, and generally the restoration or maintenance of confidence in the monetary system; and

d) cooperation with other participating countries in facilitating and stimulating an increasing interchange of goods and services among the participating countries and with other countries and in reducing public and private barriers to trade among the participating countries and with other countries.

2. Taking into account Article 8 of the Convention for European Economic Cooperation looking toward the full and effective use of manpower available in the participating countries, the Military Governors will accord sympathetic consideration to proposals, including proposals made in conjunction with the International Refugee Organization, directed to the largest practicable utilization of manpower available in any of the participating countries in furtherance of the accomplishment of the purposes of this Agreement.

3. The Military Governors will take the measures which they deem appropriate and will cooperate with other participating countries, to prevent, on the part of private or public commercial enterprises, business practices or business arrangements affecting international trade which restrain competition, limit access to markets or foster monopolistic control whenever such practices or arrangements have the effect of interfering with the achievement of the joint program of European recovery.

Article III

(Guaranties)

1. During any period in which foreign private investment is permitted in the United States/United Kingdom occupied areas, the Government of the United States of America and the Military Governors will, upon the request of either party, consult respecting projects in the United States/United Kingdom occupied areas proposed by nationals of the

United States of America may appropriately make guaranties of currency transfer under Section 111 (b) (3) of the Economic Cooperation Act of 1948.

2. The Military Governors agree that if the Government of the United States of America makes payment in United States dollars to any person under such a guaranty, any Deutsche Marks or credits in Deutsche Marks, assigned or transferred to the Government of the United States of America pursuant to that section shall be recognized as property of the Government of the United States of America.

Article IV

(Local Currency)

1. The provisions of this Article shall apply with respect to all assistance which may be furnished by the Government of the United States of America under this Agreement.

2. The Military Governors will establish a special account in the Bank Deutscher Laender in the name of the Military Governors (hereinafter called the Special Account) and will make deposits in Deutsche Marks to this account as follows:

a) The unencumbered balances of the deposits made by the Military Governors pursuant to the exchange of letters between the Government of the United States of America and the Bipartite Board dated May 1, 1948 and May 14, 1948, respectively.

b) Amounts in Deutsche Marks commensurate with the indicated dollar cost to the Government of the United States of America of commodities, services, and technical information (including any costs of processing, storing, transporting, repairing, or other services incident thereto) made available to the United States/United Kingdom occupied areas by any means (other than by guaranties authorized under the Economic Cooperation Act of 1948), less, however, the amount of the deposits made pursuant to the exchange of letters referred to in sub-paragraph (a). The Government of the United States of America shall from time to time notify the Military Governors of the indicated dollar costs of any such commodities, services, and technical information, and the amounts in Deutsche Marks commensurate with such indicated dollar costs shall be determined in the following manner. Pending the establishment of an official commercial rate of exchange between the dollar and the Deutsche Mark, the Military Governors will, upon receipt of such notification, deposit in the Special Account amounts of Deutsche Marks as agreed upon between the Government of the United States and the Military Governors. Deposits in the Special Account made, upon notification by the Government of the United States after an official commercial rate of exchange has been established, will be amounts of Deutsche Marks computed at the official rate. The Military Governors may at any time advance deposits in the Special Account which shall be credited against subsequent notifications pursuant to this paragraph.

3. The Government of the United States of America will from time to time notify the Military Governors of its requirements for administrative expenditures in Deutsche Marks within the United States/United Kingdom occupied areas incident to operations under the Economic Cooperation Act of 1948, and the Military Governors will whereupon make such sums available out of any balances in the Special Account in the manner requested by the Government of the United States of America in the notification.

4. Five percent of each deposit made pursuant to this Article in respect of assistance furnished under authority of the Foreign Aid Appropriation Act, 1949, shall be allocated to the use of the Government of the United States of America for its expenditures in the United States/United Kingdom occupied areas, and sums made available pursuant to paragraph 3 of this Article shall first be charged to the amounts allocated under this paragraph.

5. The Military Governors will further make such sums of Deutsche Marks available out of any balances in the Special Account as may be required to cover costs (including port, storage, handling and similar charges) of transportation from any point of entry in the United States/United Kingdom occupied areas to the consignee's designated points of delivery in United States/United Kingdom occupied areas of such relief supplies and packages as are referred to in Article VI.

6. The Military Governors may draw upon the remaining balance in the Special Account for such purposes as may be agreed from time to time with the Government of the United States of America. In considering proposals put forward by the Military Governors for drawings from the Special Account, the Government of the United States of America will take into account the need for promoting or maintaining internal monetary and financial stabilization in the United States/United Kingdom occupied areas and for stimulating productive activity and international trade and the exploration for and development of new sources of wealth within the United States/United Kingdom occupied areas, including in particular:

a) expenditures upon projects or programs, including those which are part of a comprehensive program for the development of the productive capacity of the United States/United Kingdom occupied areas and the other participating countries, and projects or programs the external costs of which are being covered by assistance rendered by the Government of the United States of America under the Economic Cooperation Act of 1948 or otherwise;

b) expenditures upon the exploration for and development of additional production of materials which may be required in the United States of America because of deficiencies or potential deficiencies in the resources of the United States of America; and

c) effective retirement of public debt, especially debt held by banking institutions.

7. Any unencumbered balance, other than unexpended amounts allocated under paragraph 4 of this Article, remaining in the Special Account on June 30, 1952, shall be disposed of within the United States/United Kingdom occupied areas for such purposes as may hereafter be agreed between the Government of the United States of America and the Military Governors, it being understood that the agreement of the United States of America shall be subject to approval by act of joint resolution of the Congress of the United States of America.

Article V

(Access to Materials)

1. The Military Governors will facilitate the transfer to the United States of America, for stockpiling or other purposes, of materials originating in the United States of America as a result of deficiencies or potential deficiencies in its own resources, upon such reasonable terms of sale, exchange, barter or otherwise, and in such quantities, for such period of time, as may be agreed to between the Government of the United States of America and the Military Governors after due regard for the reasonable requirements of the United States/United Kingdom occupied areas for domestic use and commercial export of such materials. The Military Governors will take such specific measures as may be necessary to carry out the provisions of this paragraph, including the promotion of the increased production of such materials within the United States/United Kingdom occupied areas, and removal of any hindrances to the transfer of such materials to the United States of America. The Military Governors will, when so requested by the Government of the United States of America, enter into negotiations for detailed arrangements necessary to carry out the provisions of this paragraph.

2. The Military Governors will, when so requested by the Government of the United States of America, negotiate such arrangements as are appropriate to carry out the provisions of paragraph (9) of sub-section 115 (b) of the Economic Cooperation Act of 1948, which relates to the development and transfer of materials required by the United States of America.

3. The Military Governors, when so requested by the Government of the United States of America, will cooperate wherever appropriate to further the objectives of paragraphs 1 and 2 of this Article in respect of materials originating outside of the United States/United Kingdom occupied areas.

Article VI

(Travel Arrangements and Relief Supplies)

1. The Military Governors will cooperate with the Government of the United States of America in facilitating and encouraging the promotion and development of travel by citizens of the United States of America to and within participating countries.

2. The Military Governors will, when so desired by the Government of the United States of America, enter into negotiations for agreements (including the provision of duty-free treatment under appropriate safeguards) to facilitate the entry into the United States/United Kingdom occupied areas of supplies of relief goods donated and of relief packages originating in the United States of America and consigned to individuals residing in the United States/United Kingdom occupied areas.

Article VII

(Consultation and Transmittal of Information)

1. The Parties to this Agreement will, upon the request of either of them, consult regarding any matter relating to the application of this Agreement or to operations or arrangements carried out pursuant to this Agreement.

2. The Military Governors will communicate to the Government of the United States of America in a form and at intervals to be indicated by the latter after consultation with the Military Governors:

a) detailed information of projects, programs and measures proposed or adopted by the Military Governors to carry out the provisions of this Agreement and the General Obligations of the Convention for European Economic Cooperation;

b) full statements of operations under this Agreement, including a statement of the use of funds, commodities and services received thereunder, such statements to be made in each calendar quarter;

c) information regarding the economy of the United States/United Kingdom occupied areas and any other relevant information, necessary

111

to supplement that obtained by the Government of the United States of America from the Organization for European Economic Cooperation, which the Government of the United States of America may need to determine the nature and scope of operations under the Economic Cooperation Act of 1948, and to evaluate the effectiveness of assistance furnished or contemplated under this Agreement and generally the progress of the joint recovery program.

3. The Military Governors will assist the Government of the United States of America to obtain information relating to the materials originating in the United States/United Kingdom occupied areas referred to in Article V which is necessary to the formulation and execution of the arrangements provided for in that Article.

Article VIII

(Publicity)

1. The Government of the United States of America and the Military Governors recognize that it is in their mutual interest that full publicity be given to the objectives and progress of the joint program for European recovery and of the actions taken in furtherance of that program. It is recognized that wide dissemination of information on the progress of the program is desirable in order to develop the sense of common effort and mutual aid which are essential to the accomplishment of the objectives of the program.

2. The Government of the United States of America will encourage the dissemination of such information and will make it available to the media of public information.

3. The Military Governors will encourage the dissemination of such information both directly and in cooperation with the Organization for European Economic Cooperation. They will make such information available to the media of public information and take all practicable steps to ensure that appropriate facilities are provided for such dissemination. They will further provide other participating countries and the Organiza-

tion for European Economic Cooperation with full information on the progress of the Program for economic recovery.

4. The Military Governors will make public in the United States/United Kingdom occupied areas in each calendar quarter full statements of operations under this Agreement, including information as to the use of funds, commodities and services received.

Article IX

(Missions)

1. The Military Governors agree to receive a Special Mission for Economic Cooperation, which shall conform to any administrative arrangements established by the President of the United States of America pursuant to Section 109 (d) of the Economic Cooperation Act of 1948 and which will discharge the responsibilities of the Government of the United States of America in the United States/United Kingdom occupied areas under this Agreement.

2. The Military Governors, upon appropriate notification from the Government of the United States of America, will accord appropriate courtesies to the Special Mission and its personnel, the United States Special Representatives in Europe and his staff and the members and staff of the Joint Committee on Foreign Economic Cooperation of the Congress of the United States of America and will grant them the facilities and assistance necessary to the effective performance of their responsibilities to assure the accomplishment of the purposes of this Agreement.

3. The Military Governors, directly and through their representatives on the Organization for European Economic Cooperation, will extend full cooperation to the Special Mission of the United States Special Representative in Europe and his staff and to the members and staff of the Joint Committee. Such cooperation shall include the provision of all information and facilities necessary to the observation and review of the carrying out of this Agreement, including the use of assistance furnished under it.

Article X

(Definitions)

As used in this Agreement:

1. The "United States/United Kingdom occupied areas" means those areas of Germany occupied by the armed forces of the United States of America and the United Kingdom.

2. The "Military Governors" means the United States and United Kingdom Military Governors in Germany.

3. The term "participating country" means

i) any country which signed the Report of the Committee of European Economic Cooperation at Paris on September 22, 1947, and territories for which it has international responsibility and to which the Economic Cooperation Agreement concluded between that country and the Government of the United States of America has been applied, and

ii) any other country (including any of the zones of occupation of Germany, and areas under international administration or control, and the Free Territory of Trieste or either of its zones) wholly or partly in Europe, together with dependent areas under its administration;

for so long as such country is a party to the Convention for European Economic Cooperation and adheres to a joint program for European recovery designed to accomplish the purposes of this Agreement.

Article XI

(Entry Into Force, Amendment, Duration)

1. This Agreement shall become effective on this day's date. Subject to the provisions of paragraphs 2 and 3 of this Article, it shall remain in force until June 30, 1953, and, unless at least six months before June 30, 1953, either the Government of the United States of America or the Military Governors shall have given notice in writing to the other of intention to terminate the Agreement on that date, it shall remain in force thereafter until the expiration of six months from the date on which such notice shall have been given.

114

2. If, during the life of this Agreement, the Government of the United States of America or the Military Governors should consider there has been a fundamental change in the basic assumptions underlying this Agreement, the other Contracting Party shall be notified in writing and the Contracting Parties will thereupon consult with a view to agreeing upon the amendment, modification or termination of this Agreement. If, after three months from such notification, the Contracting Parties have not agreed upon the action to be taken in the circumstances, either Contracting Party may give notice in writing to the other of intention to terminate this Agreement. Then, subject to the provisions of paragraph 3 of this Article, this Agreement shall terminate either:

a) six months after the date of such notice of intention to terminate, or

b) after such shorter period as may be agreed to be sufficient to ensure that the obligations of the Military Governors are performed in respect of any assistance which may continue to be furnished by the Government of the United States of America after the date of such notice;

provided, however, that Article V and paragraph 3 of Article VII shall remain in effect until two years after the date of such notice of intention to terminate, but not later than June 30, 1953.

3. Subsidiary agreements and arrangements negotiated pursuant to this Agreement may remain in force beyond the date of termination of this Agreement and the period of effectiveness of such subsidiary agreements and arrangements shall be governed by their own terms. Article IV shall remain in effect until all the sums in Deutsche Marks required to be deposited in accordance with its own terms have been disposed of as provided in that Article. Paragraph 2 of Article III shall remain in effect for so long as the guaranty payments referred to in that Article may be made by the Government of the United States of America.

4. This Agreement may be amended at any time by agreement between the Parties.

5. The Annex to this Agreement forms an integral part thereof.

6. This Agreement shall be registered with the Secretary-General of the United Nations.

IN WITNESS WHEREOF the respective representatives, duly authorized for the purpose, have signed the present Agreement.

DONE at Berlin, Germany, in duplicate, both texts authentic, this 14th day of July 1948.

Brian H. Robertson
General
Military Governor
British Zone

Lucius D. Clay
General, U. S. Army
Military Governor
United States Zone

Robert D. Murphy
United States Political Adviser
for Germany

ANNEX

Interpretative Notes

1. It is understood that the requirements of paragraph 1 (a) of Article II, relating to the adoption of measures for the efficient use of resources, would include, with respect to commodities furnished under the Agreement, effective measures, for safeguarding such commodities and for preventing their diversion to illegal or irregular markets or channels of trade.

2. It is understood that the obligation under paragraph 1 (c) of Article II to balance the Governmental budgets as soon as practicable would not preclude deficits over a short period but would mean a budgetary policy involving the balancing of the budget in the long run.

3. It is understood that the business practices and business arrangements referred to in paragraph 3 of Article II mean:

a) fixing prices, terms or conditions to be observed in dealing with others in the purchase, sale or lease of any product;

b) excluding enterprises from or allocating or dividing, any territorial market or field of business activity, or allocating customers, or fixing sales quotas or purchase quotas;

c) discriminating against particular enterprises;

d) limiting production or fixing production quotas;

e) preventing by agreement the development of application of technology or invention whether patented or unpatented;

f) extending the use of rights under patents, trade marks or copyrights granted by either Party to this Agreement to matters which, according to its laws and regulations, are not within the scope of such grants, or to products or conditions of production, use or sale which are likewise not the subjects of such grants;

g) such other practices as the Parties to this Agreement may agree to include.

4. It is understood that the Military Governors are obligated to take action in particular instances in accordance with paragraph 3 of Article II only after appropriate investigation or examination.

5. It is understood that the phrase in Article V "after due regard for the reasonable requirements of the United States/United Kingdom occupied areas for domestic use" would include the maintenance of reasonable stocks of the materials concerned and that the phrase "commercial export" might include barter transactions. It is also understood that arrangements negotiated under Article V might appropriately include provision for consultation, in accordance with the principles of Article 32 of the Havana Charter for an International Trade Organization, in the event that stockpiles are liquidated.

6. It is understood that the Military Governors will not be requested, under paragraph 2 (a) of Article VII, to furnish detailed information about minor projects or confidential commercial or technical information the disclosure of which would injure legitimate commercial interests.

7. It is understood that the relevant information required to be communicated to the Government of the United States of America under paragraph 2 (c) of Article VII will include monthly financial and operating statements of the Joint Export Import Agency and its successors.

8. It is understood that a change or prospective change in the fundamental relationship of the Military Governors of the United States/United Kingdom occupied areas would constitute a fundamental change in the basic assumptions underlying the Agreement, referred to in paragraph 2 of Article XI.

It is recognized that the provisions of the Agreement take adequate account of the basic governmental position and functions of the United States and the United Kingdom in their capacity as occupying powers in Germany. It is understood that the Agreement would not prejudice any inter-government agreement, relating to Germany among the occupying powers.

ECONOMIC COOPERATION AGREEMENT BETWEEN THE GOVERNMENT OF THE UNITED STATES OF AMERICA AND THE GOVERNMENT OF THE FEDERAL REPUBLIC OF GERMANY

On March 28, 1951, the following agreement between the United States of America and the Federal Republic of Germany was concluded, amending the Economic Cooperation Agreement published in the Supplement to the Eighth Report to Congress of the Economic Cooperation Administration on pages 14—30

APO 757-A, Frankfurt

February 27, 1951.

EXCELLENCY:

I have the honor to refer to the conversations which have recently taken place between representatives of our two governments relating to the Economic Cooperation Agreement between the United States of America and the Federal Republic of Germany, signed at Bonn on December 15th, 1949, and to the enactment into law of Public Law 535, 81st Congress, amending the Economic Cooperation Act of 1948. I also have the honor to confirm the understandings reached as a result of these conversations:

1. The Government of the Federal Republic of Germany has expressed its adherence to the principles and policies of the Economic Cooperation Act of 1948, as heretofore amended.

2. Whenever reference is made in any of the articles of such Economic Cooperation Agreement to the Economic Cooperation Act of 1948 it shall be construed as meaning the Economic Cooperation Act of 1948, as heretofore amended.

3. Paragraph 6 of Article IV shall include expenditures in furtherance of any central institution or other organization formed by two or more participating countries to facilitate the development of transferability of European currencies or to promote liberalization of trade by participating countries with one another and with other countries.

119

4. The consultation referred to in Article III, paragraph 1, shall refer to all guaranties authorized under Section 111 (b) (3) of the Economic Cooperation Act of 1948, as heretofore amended.

Accept, Excellency, the renewed assurances of my distinguished consideration.

John J. McCloy
U.S. High Commissioner for Germany

HIS EXCELLENCY
THE CHANCELLOR OF THE FEDERAL REPUBLIC OF GERMANY
Palais Schaumburg
141 Koblenzer Straße, Bonn, Germany

FEDERAL REPUBLIC OF GERMANY
OFFICE OF THE CHANCELLOR

304-06/80 II/3365/51

Bonn, 28 March 1951

MR. HIGH COMMISSIONER:

In your letter of 27 February 1951 you refer to the conversations which have recently taken place between representatives of our two governments relating to the Economic Cooperation Agreement between the United States of America and the Federal Republic of Germany, signed at Bonn on 15 December 1949, and to the enactment into law of Public Law 535, 81st Congress, amending the Economic Cooperation Act of 1948, and inform me that in the following points understanding has been reached:

1. The Government of the Federal Republic of Germany has expressed its adherence to the principles and policies of the Economic Cooperation Act of 1948, as heretofore amended.

2. Whenever reference is made in any of the articles of such Economic Cooperation Agreement to the Economic Cooperation Act of 1948 it shall be construed as meaning the Economic Cooperation Act of 1948, as heretofore amended.

3. Paragraph 6 of Article IV shall include expenditures in furtherance of any central institution or other organization formed by two or more participating countries to facilitate the development of transferability of European currencies or to promote liberalization of trade by participating countries with one another and with other countries.

4. The consultation referred to in Article III, paragraph 1, shall refer to all guaranties authorized under Section 111 (b) (3) of the Economic Cooperation Act of 1948, as heretofore amended.

I have the honor of acknowledging hereby the receipt of this letter and of informing you that I agree to its contents.

I beg Your Excellency to accept the assurance of my highest esteem.

Adenauer

HIS EXCELLENCY

Mr. John J. McCloy
U.S. High Commissioner
Bonn-Petersberg

Extract from First Report to Congress of the Economic Cooperation Administration, 9 April 1948 to 30 June 1948.

SELECTED BIBLIOGRAPHY

A b b o t t , Charles C., *The International Position and Commitments of the United States* (No. 449 in the National Economic Problems Series) American Enterprise Association, Inc., Washington, 1953

B r o w n , William A. Jr. & Opie, Redevers, *American Assistance*, Washington, The Brookings Institution, 1953

C l a y , Lucius D., *Decision in Germany*, New York, Doubleday, 1950

Congressional Record: 80th, 81st, 82nd and 83rd Sessions, *Reports and Debates on European Foreign Aid*, Washington, U.S. Government Printing Office, 1948, 1949, 1950, 1951, 1952

Economic Aid to Europe — *The Marshall Plan*, Summers, Robert E., Washington, U.S. Government Printing Office, 1947

Economic Cooperation Administration: *A Report on Recovery Progress and United States Aid*, Washington, U.S. Government Printing Office, 1949

Economic Cooperation Administration: Reports to Congress, 1st to 13th, April/June 1948 to April/June 1951, Washington, U.S. Government Printing Office, 1948—1952, 15 Volumes

European Recovery Program: Second Report of the Organization for European Economic Cooperation, Paris, 1950

Foreign Aid by the United States Government, United States Office of Business Economics, Washington, U.S. Government Printing Office 1951

P a l y i , Melchior, *The Dollar Dilemma — Perpetual Aid to Europe?* Chicago, Henry Regnery Co., 1954

President of the United States: Report to *Congress on Mutual Security Program,* 17 volumes issued every six months from 1952, Washington, U.S. Government Printing Office

Recovery under the Marshall Plan, 1948—1954; Reports of the German Government on the Progress of the Marshall Plan. A series of reports from 1948 — Bonn, Germany

Report to Congress on the *United States Foreign Aid Program,* from December 1947 on, issued in the Congressional series, House Documents, Washington, U.S. Government Printing Office

S e n n h o l z , Hans, *How Can Europe Survive?* New York, Van Nostrand Co., 1955

Task Force of Overseas Economic Operations, (Henning W. Prentis, Jr. Chairman) *Report* prepared for the Hoover Commission on Organization of the Executive Branch of Government, Washington, U.S. Government Printing Office, 1955

Three Years of the Marshall Plan, Economic Cooperation Administration, Washington, U.S. Government Printing Office, 1952

U.S. Department of State: *Outline of the European Recovery Program,* creating the Economic Cooperation Administration and defining its work, Washington, U.S. Government Printing Office, 1948

The President's Committee on Foreign Aid, European Aid, and American Aid, Washington, U.S. Government Printing Office, 1947

ABBREVIATIONS

BIS	Bank for International Settlements, Geneva
BLS	Bank of Labor Statistics, U.S.A. Washington
BRD	Bundesrepublik Deutschland — Federal Republic of Germany
CEEC	Committee of European Economic Cooperation
cif	cost, insurance, freight
ECA	Economic Cooperation Administration
EPU	European Payments Union
ERP	European Recovery Program
FOA	Foreign Operations Administration
fob	free on board
GARIOA	Government & Relief in Occupied Areas
GATT	General Agreement on Tariffs and Trade
HICOG	High Commissioner for Germany
JEIA	Joint Export Import Agency
MDAP	Mutual Defense Assistance Program
NATO	North Atlantic Treaty Organization
OMGUS	Office of Military Government, United States
OSR	Office of Special Representative
OEEC	Organization for European Economic Cooperation
OTS	Office of Technical Services
STEG	State Collection Agency for Public Properties
U. K.	United Kingdom
UN or UNO	United Nations
UNICEF	United Nations International Childrens Emergency Fund
VWG	Bizonal Economic Area

INDEX